THE WAY OF SALVATION

MEDITATIONS FOR ATTAINING CONVERSION AND HOLINESS

From

THE COMPLETE WORKS
OF
SAINT ALPHONSUS DE LIGUORI,

DOCTOR OF THE CHURCH,

**Bishop of Saint Agatha,
and Founder of the
Congregation of the Most Holy Redeemer**

**THE ASCETICAL WORKS
Volume 2**
The Way of Salvation and of Perfection

**TRANSLATED FROM THE ITALIAN
EDITED BY
REV. EUGENE GRIMM, CSsR**

**NEW YORK, CINCINNATI, AND ST. LOUIS.
1886**

Abridged and further edited by Darrell Wright, 2017

CONTENTS (Page numbers as in original book)

NOTICE

THIS volume contains the quintessence of the science of the saints. It gives a correct idea of the spirit, of the heart, and of the talent of Saint Alphonsus: one might say that in it his whole soul is poured out.

The entire work is divided into three parts. In the first, we resume, under another form, the considerations on the eternal truths or the Last Things, treated at greater length in the preceding volume. The second part traces and paves the way that leads to divine love, or to sanctity and true happiness, and inspires us at the same time with the desire, the zeal, and the courage to undertake everything to reach this end. The third part transports us to the summit of the holy mountain, or Christian perfection, shows us in detail the mysteries of the interior life, and enables us to breathe its sweetest perfume.

Some persons have objected that the writings of Saint Alphonsus contain many repetitions. This is true in regard to the ascetical works; but these repetitions are not useless. There is no question here of a study, a scientific work done for the sole purpose of exercising the mind. It is a food destined to give strength to the life of the soul. Each one takes for himself every day the amount that agrees with his spiritual temperament. But let us hear what the author himself says in regard to this matter: "I entreat my readers not to grow weary if in those prayers they always find petitions for the grace of perseverance and the grace of divine love. For us, these are the two graces most necessary for the attainment of eternal salvation."**1** He also says: "One should not find it tiresome that I repeat the texts that I have already cited several times. . . . The authors of pernicious books, who treat of obscene things, reproduce even to satiety their impure assaults in order to inflame their imprudent readers with the fire of concupiscence; and should it not be permitted to me to repeat sacred texts that are most suitable to inflame souls with divine love?"**2** Let us never grow tired of reading and meditating on what the holy bishop has have the patience to write so many times for our benefit. ED.

1 *Preparation for Death*. Preface.
2 Consideration on the Passion, ch. 8.

MEDITATION 1.
Eternal Salvation.

1. Our most important affair is that of our eternal
salvation; upon it depends our happiness or misery forever. This affair will come to an end in eternity, and
will decide whether we shall be saved or lost forever;
whether we shall have acquired an eternity of delights,
or an eternity of torments; whether we shall live forever
happy, or forever miserable.

O God! what will my lot be? Shall I be saved, or
shall I be lost? I may be either. And if I may be lost,
why do I not embrace such a life, as may secure for
me life eternal? O Jesus! You died to save me; yet
I have been lost, as often as I have lost You, my sovereign good: permit me not to lose You any more.
[16] Men esteem it a great affair to gain a lawsuit, to
obtain a post of honor, or to acquire an estate. Nothing, however, that will end with time deserves to be
esteemed great. Since, therefore, all the goods of this
world will one day end for us, as we shall either
leave them or they will leave us, that affair alone should
be esteemed great upon which depends eternal happiness or eternal misery.

O Jesus, my Redeemer, cast me not away from Your
face, as I have deserved! I am indeed a sinner; but I
am grieved from the bottom of my heart for having

offended Your infinite goodness. Until now I have despised You, but now I love You above all things. Henceforth You alone shall be my only good, my only love. Have pity on a sinner who penitently casts him self at Your feet, and desires to love You. If I have grievously offended You, I now ardently desire to love You. What would have become of me, If you had called me out of life when I had lost Your grace and favor? Since You, O Lord! have shown so much mercy to me, grant me grace to become a saint.

3. Let us awaken our faith in a heaven and a hell of eternal duration: one or other will be our lot.

O God! how could I, knowing that by committing sin I was condemning myself to eternal torments - how could I sin so often against You and forfeit Your grace? Knowing that You are my God and my Redeemer, how could I, for the sake of a miserable gratification, so often turn my back upon You? O God, I am sorry more than every evil for having thus despised You. I love You above every good, and henceforth I will suffer the loss of all things rather than lose Your friendship. Give me strength to continue faithful. And do You, O Blessed Virgin Mary! pray for me and assist me.

MEDITATION 2.
Sin as it Dishonors God.

1. *By transgression of the law You dishonor God.***1** When
the sinner deliberates whether he shall give or refuse his
consent to sin, he takes the balance into his hands to
decide which is of most value - the favor of God, some
passion, some worldly interest or pleasure. When he
yields to temptation, what does he do? He decides that
some wretched gratification is more desirable than the
favor of God. Thus it is that he dishonors God, declar-
ing, by his consent, that a miserable pleasure is prefer-
ble to the divine friendship.

Thus, then, O God! have I so many times dishonored
You, by esteeming You less than my miserable passions.

2. Of this the Almighty complains by the prophet Eze-
kiel, when he says: *They violated Me among My people,*
*for a handful of barley and a piece of bread.***2** If the sinner
should exchange God for a treasure of jewels, or for a
kingdom, it would indeed be doing a great evil, because
God is of infinitely more value than all the treasures
and kingdoms of the earth. But for what do so many
exchange him? for a vapor, for a little dirt, for a pois-
oned pleasure, which is no sooner tasted than it vanishes.

God! how could I have have the heart for such vile
things, so often to despise You, who have shown so

much love for me? But behold, my Redeemer, how I
now love You above all things; and because I love You,
I feel more regret for having lost You, my God, than if
I had lost all other goods, and even my life. Have pity
on me, and forgive me. I will never more incur Your

1 "Per praevaricationem legis, Deum inhonoras." Rom. 2.23.
2 "Violabant me . . . propter pugillum hordei et fragmen panis."
Ezek. 13.19.

displeasure. Grant that I may rather die than offend
You any more.

3. *Lord, who is like You?*[1] And what good things, O
God! can be comparable to You, O infinite goodness?
But how could I have turned my back upon You, to give
myself to those vile things which sin held out to me? O
Jesus, Your precious blood is my hope. You have promised to hear him who prays to You. I ask You not
for the goods of this world: I ask You for the pardon
of those sins which I have committed against You, and
for which I am sorry above every other evil. I ask You
for perseverance in Your grace until the end of my life.

I ask You for the gift of Your holy love; my soul is en-
amored of Your goodness; hear me, O Lord! Only grant
that I may love You both here and hereafter, and to all
things else do with me as You please. My Lord, and
my only good, permit me not to be any more separated
from You! Mary, Mother of God, do You also listen to

me, and obtain for me that I may ever belong to God, and that God may be my inheritance forever.

MEDITATION 3.
The Patience of God in waiting for Sinners.

1. Who in this world has so much patience with his equals as God with us his creatures, in bearing with us, and waiting for our repentance, after the many offenses we have committed against him?

Ah! my God, had I thus offended my brother or my father, long ago would he have driven me from his face! O Father of mercies, cast me not away from Your face, but have pity on me.

2. You have mercy, says the wise man, upon all, because *You can do all things, and overlook the sins of men for the*

1 "Domine, quis similis tibi?" Ps. 34.10.
2 "Ne projicias me a facie tua." Ps. 1.13.

[19] *sake of repentance.***1** Men conceal their sense of the injuries which they receive, either because they are good, and know that it belongs not to themselves to punish those who offend them; or because they are unable, and have not the power to revenge themselves. But to You, my God, it does belong to take revenge for the offenses

which are committed against Your infinite majesty; and You indeed are able to avenge Yourself, whenever You please; and do You dissemble? Men despise You; they make promises to You and afterwards betray You; and You seem not to behold them, or as if You have little concern for Your honor?

Thus, O Jesus, have You done towards me. Ah! my God, my infinite good, I will no longer despise You, I will no longer provoke You to chastise me. And why should I delay until You abandon me in reality and condemn me to hell? I am truly sorry for all my offenses against You. I would rather have died than offend You! You are my Lord, You have created me, and You have redeemed me by Your death; You alone have loved, You alone deserve to be loved, and You alone shall be the sole object of my love.

3. My soul, how could you be so ungrateful and so daring against your God? When you offended him, could he not have suddenly called you out of life and punished you with hell? And yet he waited for you; instead of chastising you, he preserved your life and gave you good things. But you, instead of being grateful to him and loving him for such excessive goodness, you continued to offend him!

O my Lord, since You have waited for me with so great mercy, I give You thanks. I am sorry for having

offended You. I love You. I might at this hour have
dwelt in hell, where I could not have repented, nor have

1 "Misereris omnium, quia omnia potes; et dissimulas peccata
hominum propter poenitentiam." Wis. 11.24.

[20] loved You. But now that I can repent, I grieve with
my whole heart for having offended Your infinite goodness; and I love You above all things, more than I love
myself. Forgive me, and grant that from this day I may
love no other but You, who have so loved me. May I
live for You alone, my Redeemer, who for me did die
upon the cross! All my hopes are in Your bitter Passion.
O Mary, Mother of God! assist me by Your holy intercession.

MEDITATION 4.
The Certainty of Death.

1. We must die! how awful is the decree! we must die.
The sentence is passed: *It is appointed for all men once to
die.*1 You are a man and You must die. St. Cyprian says
that we are born with a rope around our necks, and as long
as we live on earth we hourly approach the gallows, that
is, the sickness that puts an end to our life. It would
be madness for any one to delude himself with the idea
that he shall not die. A poor man may flatter himself
that he may become rich, or a vassal that he may be a

king; but who can ever hope to escape death? One dies old, another young, but all at last must come to the grave.

I therefore must one day die and enter eternity. But what will be my lot for eternity? happy or miserable? My Savior Jesus, be You a Savior to me!

2. Of all those who were living upon the earth at the beginning of the last century, not one is now alive. The greatest and most renowned princes of this world have exchanged their country; scarcely does there remain any remembrance of them, and their bare bones are hardly preserved in stone monuments.

Make me, O God! more and more sensible of the folly

1 "Statutum est hominibus semel mori." Heb. 9.27.

[21] of loving the goods of this world, and for the sake of them renouncing You, my sovereign and infinite good. What folly have I not been guilty of; and how much it grieves me! I give You thanks for having made me sensible of it.

3. A hundred years from here, at most, and neither you nor I will be any longer in this world; both will have gone into the house of eternity. A day, an hour, a moment, is approaching which will be the last both for you

and me; and this hour, this moment, is already fixed by Almighty God; how then can we think of anything else but of loving God, who will then be our judge?

Alas! what will my death be? O my Jesus and my judge! what will become of me when I shall have to appear before You to give an account of my whole life? Pardon me, I beseech You, before that moment arrives which will decide my happiness or misery for eternity. I am sorry for having offended You, my sovereign good. Until now I have not loved You; but now I will love You with my whole soul. Grant me the grace of perseverance. O Mary, refuge of sinners, have pity on me!

MEDITATION 5.
The Loss of all Things in Death.

1. *The day of destruction is at hand.*[1] The day of death is called the day of destruction, because then is destroyed all that man has acquired; honors, friends, riches, possessions, kingdoms - all are then no more. What then does it profit us to gain the whole world if in death we must leave all? All is at an end at the bedside of the dying man. Is there any king, do you think, said St. Ignatius to Xavier when he sought to bring him to God, who has taken with him into the other world even a thread of purple to mark his sovereignty? Has any rich

1 "Juxta est dies perditionis." Deut. 32.35.

[22] man taken with him a single coin, or even one servant to attend him? In death all is left behind. The soul enters eternity alone and unattended, except by its works.

Woe to me! where are my works to accompany me to a blessed eternity? I can discover none but such as render me deserving of eternal torments.

2. Men come into the world in unequal conditions: one is born rich, another poor, one a noble, another a plebean; but all go out of it equal and alike. Consider the graves of the dead: see if you can discover among the bodies which are there interred, who was a master and who a servant, who was a king and who a beggar.

O God! while others amass the fortunes of this world, may my only fortune be Your holy grace. You alone are my only good both in this life and in the next.

3. In one word, everything on earth will come to an end. All greatness will end, all misery will end, honors will end, misery will end; pleasures will end, sufferings will end. Blessed in death, therefore, not he who has abounded in riches, honors, and pleasures, but he who has patiently endured poverty, contempt, and sufferings! The possession of temporal goods affords no consolation at the moment of death: that alone consoles us which has been done or suffered for God.

O Jesus! separate my heart from this world, before death entirely takes me from it. Help me with Your grace; You indeed know how great is my weakness. Permit me not to be any more unfaithful to You, as I have until now been. I am sorry, O Lord! for having so often despised You. Now will I love You above every good, and will die a thousand times rather than forfeit Your grace. But the infernal one ceases not to tempt me; in mercy abandon me not, leave me not to myself, permit me not to be any more separated from Your love. O Mary, my hope! obtain for me the grace of perseverance.

[23] **MEDITATION 6.**
The Great thought of Eternity.

1. Thus did St. Augustine designate the thought of eternity: "The great thought" -- "*magna cogitatio*." It was this thought that induced so many solitaries to retire into deserts; so many religious, even kings and queens, to shut themselves up in cloisters; and so many martyrs to sacrifice their lives in the midst of torments, in order to acquire a happy eternity in heaven, and to avoid a miserable eternity in hell. The Ven. John of Avila converted a certain lady with these two words: "Reflect," said he to her, "on these two words: *Forever* and *Never*." A certain monk went down into a grave that he might meditate continually on eternity, and con-

stantly repeated, "O eternity! eternity!"

How frequently, my God, have I deserved the eternity of hell! Oh, that I had never offended You! Grant me sorrow for my sins; have compassion on me.

2. The same Ven. John of Avila says that he who believes in eternity and becomes not a saint should be confined as one deranged. He who builds a house for himself takes great pains to make it comfortable, spacious, and handsome, and says: "I labor and give myself a great deal of trouble about this house, because I shall have to live in it all my life." And yet how little is the house of eternity thought of! When we shall have arrived at eternity there will be no question of our residing in a house more or less comfortable, or more or less spacious: the question will be of our dwelling in a palace overflowing with delights, or in a gulf of endless torments. And for how long a time? not for forty or fifty years, but forever, as long as God shall be God. The saints, to obtain salvation, thought it little to give their [24] whole lives to prayer, penance, and the practice of good works. And what do we do for the same end?

O my God! many years of my life are already past, already death is near at hand, and what good have I until now done for You? Give me light, and strength, to devote the remainder of my days to Your service. Too much, alas! have I offended You; I desire from henceforth to love You.

3. *With fear and trembling work out your salvation.***1**
To obtain salvation we must tremble at the thought of
being lost, and tremble not so much at the Thought of
hell, as of sin, which alone can send us there. He who
dreads sin avoids dangerous occasions, frequently recom-
mends himself to God, and has recourse to the means
of keeping himself in the state of grace. He who acts
thus will be saved; but for him who lives not in this
manner it is morally impossible to be saved. Let us
attend to that saying of St. Bernard: "We cannot be too
secure where eternity is at stake."**2**

Your blood, O Jesus, my Redeemer! is my security. I
should have been already lost on account of my sins,
had You not offered me Your pardon, on condition of
my repentance for having offended You. I am sorry
therefore with my whole heart for having offended You,
who are infinite goodness. I love You, O sovereign
good! above every other good, I know that You will
 my salvation, and I will endeavor to secure it by
loving You forever. O Mary, Mother of God! pray to
Jesus for me.

MEDITATION 7.
The Death of Jesus Christ.

1. How is it possible to believe that the Creator should

have been willing to die for us, his creatures? Yet we

1 "Cum metu et tremore vestram salutem operamini." Phil. 2.12.
2 Nulla nimis securitas, ubi periclitatur aeternitas.

[25] must believe it because faith so teaches it. Hence the Council of Nice commands us to confess: "I believe in one Lord Jesus Christ, the Son of God, who for us men and for our salvation was crucified for us, suffered, and was buried."

And if it is true, O God of love! that You have died for the love of men, can there be one who believes this, and does not love You, so loving a God? But, O God! of those who are guilty of such ingratitude I am one; and not only have I not loved You, my Redeemer, but I have many times, for the sake of gratifying my miserable and depraved inclinations, renounced Your grace and Your love.

2. You have then, my Lord and my God, died for me; and how could I, knowing this, have so often disowned You and turned my back upon You? But You, my Savior, came down from heaven to save that which was lost.2 My ingratitude, therefore, does not deprive me of the hope of pardon. Yes, O Jesus! I hope that You will pardon me all offenses which I have committed against You, through the death which You did suffer for me on Mount Cal-

vary. Oh that I could die of grief and of love as often as I think of the offenses which I have committed against the love which You have shown towards me! Make known to me, O Lord! what I must do henceforward to make amends for my ingratitude. Keep up in my mind a continual remembrance of the bitter death You were pleased to suffer for me, that I may love You and never more offend You.

3. God, then, has died for me; and shall I be able to

1 Credo ... in unum Dominum Jesum Christum, Filium Dei . . . qui propter nos homines, et propter nostram salutem . . . crucifixus . . . passus et sepultus est.
2 "Venit enim Filius hominis salvare quod perierat." Matt. 18.11.

[26] love anything else but God? No, my Jesus, I will love none but You. You have loved me too much. You can do no more to compel me to love You. I have obliged You by my sins to cast me away from Your face; but You have not abandoned me forever; You regard me with tender affection; You are about to call me to Your love; I will no longer resist. I love You, my sovereign good; I love You, my God, who are worthy of infinite love; I love You, my God, who have died for me. I love You, but I love You not enough; do You increase my love. Grant that I may forsake all things, and forget all things else, to please and to love You, my Redeemer, my love, and my all. O Mary, my hope! recommend me to Your divine Son.

MEDITATION 8.
The Abuse of God's Mercy.

1. There are two ways by which the devil endeavors
to deceive men to their eternal ruin: after they have committed sin he tempts them to despair on account of the
severity of divine justice; but before they have sinned
he encourages them to do so by the hope of obtaining
the divine mercy. And he effects the ruin of numberless
souls as well by the second as by the first artifice. "God
is merciful," says the obstinate sinner to him who would
convert him from the iniquity of his ways. "God is
merciful." But as the Mother of God expresses it in
her canticle, *His mercy is to them that fear Him.***1** Yes, the
Lord deals mercifully with him that fears to offend him,
but not so with the man who presumes upon his mercy
to offend him still more.

O God! I give You thanks for having made me sensible
of Your patience in bearing with me. Behold, I am of

1 "Misericordia ejus timentibus eum." Luke 1.50.

[27] the number of those who, presuming on Your goodness, have offended You again and again.

2. God is merciful; but he is also just. Sinners are desirous that he should be merciful only, without being just;
but that is impossible, because if he were only to for-

give and never to chastise, he would be lacking in justice. Hence Father Avila observes that patience on the part of God towards those who avail themselves of his mercy just to offend him the more, would not be mercy, but a lack of justice. He is bound to chastise the ungrateful. He bears with them for a certain time, but after that abandons them.

Such a punishment, O God! has not as yet overtaken me, or else I would have now dwelt in hell, or been obstinate in my sins. But no: I desire to amend my life; I desire to offend You no more. Though I have until now displeased You, I am sorry for it with my whole soul; I desire henceforth to love You, and I desire to love You more than others do, because You have not shown the same patience towards others as towards me.

3. *God is not mocked.***1** Yet he would be mocked, if the sinner could go on continually offending him, and yet afterwards enjoy him in heaven. *What things a man shall sow, those also shall he reap.***2** He who sows good works shall reap rewards; but he who sows iniquities shall reap chastisements. The hope of those who commit sin because God is forgiving is an abomination in his sight: *their hope*, says holy Job, *is an abomination.***3** Hence the sinner, by such hope, provokes God to chastise him the sooner, as that servant would provoke his master, who, because his master was good, took advantage of his goodness to behave badly.

O Jesus! such, I fear, has been my conduct towards You;

1 "Deus non irridetur." Gal. 6.7.
2 "Quae seminaverit homo, haec et metet." Gal. 6.8.
3 "Spes illorum abominatio." Job 11.20.

[28] because You were good I have made no account of Your precepts. I confess that I have done wickedly; and I detest all the offenses I have committed against You. Now do I love You more than myself, and I desire never more to displease You. Ah, if I should again offend You by mortal sin! Permit it not, O Lord; rather let me die. O Mary, Mother of perseverance, do assist me!

MEDITATION 9.
The Emptiness and Shortness of Human Life.

1. Holy David said that the happiness of this life is as the dream of one awaking from sleep: *as the dream of them that awake.*1 All the greatness and glory of this world will appear no more to poor wordlings at the hour of death, than as a dream to one awaking from sleep, who finds that the fortune which he has acquired in his dream ends with his sleep. Hence, did one who was undeceived wisely write on the skull of a dead man, "*Cogitanti omnia vilescunt.*" "He who thinks will undervalue all things." Yes, to him who thinks on death, all the goods of this life appear as they really are, vile and transitory. Nor can that man

fix his affections on the earth who reflects that in a short time he must leave it forever.

Ah, my God, how often have I despised Your grace for the miserable goods of this world! Henceforth I desire to think of nothing but of loving and serving You. Assist me with Your holy grace.

2. "And is it thus, then, that worldly grandeur and sovereign power must end?" Such was the exclamation of St. Francis Borgia, when he beheld the corpse of the Empress Isabella, who died in the flower of her youth. Reflecting upon what he saw, he resolved to bid adieu to the world, and to give himself entirely to God, say-

1 "Velut somnium surgentium." Ps. 72.20.

[29] ing, "I will henceforth serve a master who will never forsake me." Let us detach ourselves from present goods before death tears us away from them. What folly it is to expose ourselves to the danger of losing our souls, for the sake of some attachment to this miserable world, from which we shall soon have to depart; for soon it will be said to us by the minister of God, "*Go forth, Christian soul, out of this world!*"

O my Jesus, if only I had always loved You! How many offenses have I been guilty of against You! Teach me how to correct my disorderly life, for I am

willing to do whatever You please. Accept my love, accept my repentance, in which I love You more than myself, and crave Your mercy and compassion.
3. Reflect that you cannot remain forever in this world. You must one day leave the country in which you now reside; you must one day go out from the house in which you now dwell to return to it no more.

Make me sensible, O God, of the injustice I have been guilty of in turning my back upon You, my sovereign good; and grant me the sorrow to bewail my ingratitude as I ought. O that I had died rather than ever offended You! Do not allow me to live any longer ungrateful for the love which You have shown me. My dear Redeemer, I love You above all things, and I desire to love You to the best of my power during the remainder of life. Strengthen my weakness by Your grace; and do You, Mary, Mother of God, intercede for me.

1 Proficiscere, anima Christiana, de hoc mundo.

[30] **MEDITATION 10.**
The Contempt with which the Sinner treats God.

1. God himself declares that the sinner treats him with contempt, and complains of it in these words: I have brought up children, and exalted them; but they have despised me.**1** I have brought up my children, I have pre-

served and nourished them, but with base ingratitude they have despised me. But who is God who is thus despised by men? He is the Creator of heaven and earth; he is the sovereign infinite good, in whose sight men and angels are as a drop of water, or a grain of sand: *as a drop of a bucket, as a little dust.*2 In a word, all things created, in the presence of his infinite greatness, are as though they were not: *All nations are before him as if they have no being at all, and counted to him nothing and vanity.*3

Behold me, O God! a daring sinner who have presumed to despise Your infinite majesty. But while You are infinite majesty, You are also infinite mercy. I love You, O Lord! and because I love You I am sorry for having offended You; have pity on me.

2. And, O God! who am I who have despised You? A poor helpless worm, who have nothing but what You in Your bounty have bestowed upon me. You have given me my soul, my body, the use of reason, and numberless other benefits in this world; and I have made no other use of them all but to offend You, my benefactor. Nay, more; at the very time that You did preserve my life, that I might not fall into hell as I deserved, I abused Your goodness and forbearance. O my Savior! how could You have had such patience with me? Wretch

1 "Filios enutrivi et exaltavi; ipsi autem spreverunt me." Isaiah 1.2.

2 "Quasi stilla situlae . . . quasi pulvis exiguus." Isaiah 40.15.
3 "Omnes gentes quasi non sint, sic sunt coram eo." Isaiah 40.17.

[31] that I am, how many nights I slept under Your displeasure! But You would not have me perish. I trust, O my Jesus! in Your blessed Passion that You will enable me to change my life. Let not that sacred blood be lost, which with so much pain and sorrow You shed for my salvation.

3. But, O God! what have I done! You, my Redeemer, have shown that regard for my soul, so as to shed Your blood for its salvation, and I have been so wretched as to allow it to perish for a mere nothing, for a whim, for a maddening passion, for a miserable gratification, for contempt of Your grace and love. Ah! if faith did not assure me that You have promised to pardon those who repent, I should not now dare to implore Your forgiveness. O my Savior! I kiss Your sacred wounds, and for the love of these wounds I beseech You to forget the injuries which I have committed against You. You have said that, when the sinner repents, You will forget all his ingratitude. I am sorry above every evil for having despised You, my sovereign good; make haste to pardon me, as You have promised; let me be quickly reconciled to You. I love You now more than myself; may I never more incur Your displeasure. O Mary, refuge of sinners! attend to a poor sinner who invokes Your assistance.

MEDITATION 11.
The Pain of Loss.

1. The greatest pain of hell is not the fire nor the darkness, not the stench, nor any other of all the material torments of that dreadful prison of despair; it is the pain of loss - that is, the pain of having lost God which of itself may be said to constitute hell. The soul was created to be forever united with God, and to enjoy the sight of his enrapturing countenance. God is its last [32] end, its only good, so that all the goods of earth and heaven, without God, could not make it happy. Hence it is that if a condemned soul in hell could possess and love God, hell, with all its torments, would be to it a paradise. But this will be its greatest punishment, which will render it forever inconceivably miserable, to be deprived of God for all eternity, without the least hope of ever again beholding him or loving him.

Jesus, my Redeemer! nailed to the cross for my sake, You are my hope; oh that I had died rather than offended You!

2. The soul, being created for God, has an instinctive tendency to become united with its sovereign good, its God; but being united with the body, when it wallows in iniquity, it becomes so darkened by the created objects which allure the senses that it loses its sight, and has so little knowledge of God as no longer to desire to

be united with him. But when separated from the body, and from sensible objects, then it will know that God is the only good that can render it happy. Therefore, as soon as it shall have departed from here, it will feel itself drawn with most powerful attraction towards a union with God; but having left this life an enemy of God, it will be not only kept back from him by its sins, as by a chain, but dragged by them into hell, there to be forever separated and at a distance from God. The wretched soul in that eternal dungeon will know how beautiful God is, but will not be able to behold him. It will know how amiable God is, but will not be able to love him; it will even feel itself forced by its sins to hate him; and this will be its hell of hells, to know that it hates a God who is infinitely lovely. It will desire that it were possible to destroy God, to whom it is hateful; and to destroy itself, hating God; and this will be the eternal occupation of this unhappy soul.

O Lord! have pity on me.

[33] 3. This torment will be immensely increased by the remembrance of the graces that God bestowed upon it, and the love which he evinced towards it during its lifetime. It will especially call to mind the love of Jesus Christ in shedding his blood, and laying down his life for its salvation; but, ungrateful soul, not to forego its own miserable gratifications, it consented to lose God, its sovereign good; and it will find that no hope will be

left of ever regaining him.

Ah, my God! If I were in hell, I would not be able to love You, nor to repent of my sins; but as I have it now in my power to repent and to love You, I am sorry with my whole soul for having offended You, and love You above all things. Grant me to remember continually that hell which I have deserved, that I may love You with still greater and greater fervor. O Mary, refuge of sinners! do not abandon me.

MEDITATION 12.
The Particular Judgment.

1. *It is appointed unto men once to die, and after this the judgment.***1** It is of faith, that immediately after death we shall be judged according to our works in this life. And it is also of faith, that upon this judgment will depend our eternal salvation or perdition. Imagine yourself to be in your agony, and to have only a short time to live. Think that in a short time you would then have to appear before Jesus Christ to give an account of your whole life. Alas! how alarming would the sight of your sins then be to you!

Jesus, my Redeemer! pardon me, I beseech You, before You judge me. I know that I have many times

1 "Statutum est hominibus semel mori; post hoc autem, judicium."

Heb. 9.27.

[34] already deserved to be sentenced to eternal death.
No, I desire not to present myself guilty before You, but
penitent and pardoned. O my sovereign good! I am
grievously sorry for having offended You.

2. O God! what will be the anguish of the soul when
it shall first behold Jesus Christ as its judge, and behold
him terrible in his wrath? It will then see how much
he has suffered for its sake; it will see what great
mercies he has exercised towards it, and what powerful
means he has bestowed upon it for the attainment of
salvation; then will it also see the greatness of eternal
goods, and the vileness of earthly pleasures, which have
wrought its ruin; it will then see all these things, but to
no purpose, because then there will be no more time to
correct its past errors; what shall have then been done
will be irrevocable. Before the judgment seat of God,
no nobility, nor dignity, nor riches will be considered;
our works alone will be weighed there.
Grant, O Jesus! that when I first behold You I may
see You appeased; and, for this end, grant me the grace
to weep, during the remainder of my life, over the evil
which I have done in turning my back upon You, to
follow my own sinful caprices. No, I desire never more
to offend You. I love You and desire to love You forever.

3. What contentment will that Christian enjoy at the
hour of death who has left the world to give himself to

God; who has denied his senses all unlawful gratifications: and who, if he has on some occasions been negligent,
has at last been wise enough afterwards to do worthy
penance for it! On the other hand, what anguish will
that Christian experience who has continually relapsed
into the same vices, and at last finds himself at the point
of death! Then will he exclaim: "Alas! in a few moments
I must appear before Jesus as my judge, and I have not
as yet even begun to change my life! I have many times
[35] promised to do so, but I have not done it; and now, in
a short time, what will become of me?"

Ah, my Jesus and my judge! I give You thanks for
the patience with which You have until now waited for
me. How many times have I myself written my own
eternal condemnation . Since You have thus waited to
pardon me, reject me not, now prostrate at Your feet.
Receive me into Your favor through the merits of Your
bitter Passion. I am sorry, my sovereign good! for having despised You. I love You above all things. I desire never more to forsake You. O Mary! recommend
me to Your Son Jesus, and do not abandon me.

MEDITATION 13.
Preparation for the Particular Judgment

1. *Be ready: for at what hour you think not, the Son of
man will come.***1** The time of death will not be the time

to prepare ourselves to die well; to die well and happily, we must prepare ourselves beforehand. There will not be time then to eradicate bad habits from the soul, to expel from the heart its predominant passions, and to extinguish all affection to earthly goods. *The night comes when no man can work.*2 All in death will be night, when nothing will be seen; and, from here, nothing done. The heart hardened, the mind obscured, confusion, fear, the desire of health, will all render it almost impossible at the hour of death to set in order a conscience confused and entangled in sin.

Sacred wounds of my Redeemer! I adore you, I humbly kiss you, and I confide in you.

2. The saints Thought they did but little, though they spent their whole lives in preparing for death, by acts of

1 "Estote parati, quia, qua hora non putatis, Filius hominis veniet." Lk.12.40.
2 "Venit nox, quando nemo potest operari." John 9.4.

[36] penance, prayer, and the practice of good works; and they trembled when they came to die. The venerable John Avila, although he had led a very holy life from his youth, when it was announced to him that he was about to die, made answer and said, "Oh that I may have a little more time to prepare myself for death!" And what shall we say when the summons of death shall be brought to us?

No, my God, I do not wish to die troubled and ungrateful, as at present I should die, if death were to overtake me; I desire to change my life, I desire to bewail my offenses against You, I desire to love You with my whole heart. O Lord! help me, enable me to do something for You before I die, for You who have died for the love of me.

3. *The time is short,*1 says the Apostle. Yes, we have but a short time in which to set our accounts in order. Hence the Holy Spirit admonishes us, *Whatever your hand is able to do, do it quickly.*2 Whatever you are able to do today, do not put off till tomorrow; for today is passing away, and tomorrow may bring death, which will deprive you of all means of doing good, or of amending what you have done badly. Woe to me if death should find me still attached to this world!

Ah, my God, how many years have I lived at a distance from You! And how have You had so much patience with me, in waiting for me and in calling me so often to repentance! I thank You, O my Redeemer! for Your long forbearance, and I hope to thank You for it forever in heaven. *The mercies o the Lord I will sing forever.*3 Until now I have not loved You, and have made little account of being or not being loved by You, but now

1 "Tempus breve est." 1 Cor. 7.29.
2 "Quodcumque facere potest manus tua, instanter operare."
Eccles. 9.10.

3 "Misericordias Domini in aeternum cantabo." Ps. 88.2.

[37] I do love You with my whole heart; I love You above all things, more than I love myself, and I desire nothing so much as to be loved by You; and, recollecting how I have despised Your love, I would willingly die of grief for having done so. Jesus, grant me perseverance in virtue. Mary, my holy mother, obtain for me the happiness of being faithful to God.

MEDITATION 14.
The Suffering of Souls in Hell in their Mental Faculties.

1. The souls in hell will be tormented in their memory. Never, in the abode of infinite misery will they lose for a moment the remembrance of the time that was allowed them in this life to practice virtue, and to make amends for the evil which they have done; and never will it be concealed from them that there is no longer the least hope of remedy. They will call to mind the lights which they received from God, his many loving calls, his offers of pardon, all despised; and they will see that all is now at an end, and that nothing remains for them but to suffer and to despair for all eternity.

O Jesus! Your blood, Your sufferings, and Your death are my trust and hope. Alas! permit me not to fall into hell, there to curse forever even the blessings which

You have bestowed upon me.

2. The souls in hell will be tormented in their under-
standing, by thinking continually of heaven, which they
have willfully lost through their own fault. The immense felicity enjoyed by the blessed in the abode of
delights will be forever before their eyes; and this will
render their life of dreadful sufferings, which they must
endure forever in the prison of despair and woe, still
more tormenting.

If I had died, my Redeemer, when I was in sin, I
would now have no hope of ever enjoying You in
[38] heaven! You gave me life that I might gain heaven,
and now have I lost heaven for something worse than
nothing, by losing Your grace! I love You, O God, and
I am sorry for having offended You; and I hope, through
the merits of Your Passion, to come to love You forever
in heaven.

3. The souls in hell will be tormented in their will, by
being denied everything which they desire, and by having every punishment inflicted upon them which they
do not desire. They will never have anything which
they wish for, but everything which they abhor. They
will long to rid themselves of their torments and to find
peace; but there will be no peace for them; they will be
forced to dwell in the midst of their torments forever.
Their perverse will, by hating God when they know him

to be the supreme good, and worthy of infinite love, will become their greatest torment.

So it is, my God; You are an infinite good and worthy of infinite love, and I have exchanged You for nothing! Oh that I had died and had not offered You so grievous an injury! I love You, my sovereign good. Have pity on me and permit me not to be again ungrateful to You! I renounce all the delights of this world, and embrace You as my only good. I will be forever Yours; be forever mine. This is my hope, my God, my love, and my all. Deus meus et omnia. O Mary! You are all-powerful with God; obtain for me the grace of leading a holy life.

MEDITATION 15.
Devotion to the Blessed Virgin Mary.

1. Jesus is the mediator of justice; Mary obtains for us grace; for, as St. Bernard, St. Bonaventure, St. Bernardine of Siena, St. Germanus, St. Antoninus, and others say, it is the will of God to dispense through the hands [39] of Mary whatever graces he is pleased to bestow upon us. With God, the prayers of the saints are the prayers of his friends, but the prayers of Mary are the prayers of his mother. Happy they who confidently and at all times have recourse to this heavenly mother! This, above all others, is the most pleasing devotion to the Blessed

Virgin, often to have recourse to her and to say : O Mary! intercede for me with Your Son Jesus.

2. Jesus is omnipotent by nature; Mary is very powerful by grace; she obtains whatever she asks for. It is impossible, says St. Antoninus, that this mother should ask any favor of her Son for those who are devout to her, and the Son not grant her request. Jesus delights to honor his mother by granting whatever she asks of him. Hence St. Bernard exhorts us to seek for grace, and to seek for it through Mary; because she is a mother to whom nothing can be denied.1 If, then, we desire to be saved, let us recommend ourselves to Mary, that she may intercede for us, because her prayers are always heard. O mother of mercy! have pity on me. You are called the advocate of sinners; assist me, therefore, a sinner placing my confidence in You.

3. Let us not doubt whether Mary will hear us when we address our prayers to her. It is her delight to exercise her powerful influence with God in obtaining for us whatever graces we stand in need of. It is sufficient to ask favors of Mary to obtain them. If we are unworthy of them, she renders us worthy by her powerful intercession; and she is very desirous that we should have recourse to her, that she may save us. What sinner ever perished, who, with confidence and perseverance, had recourse to Mary, the refuge of sinners? He is lost who does not have recourse to Mary.

Mary, my mother and my hope! I take refuge

1 "Quaeramus gratiam, et per Mariam quaeramus; quia Mater est, et frustrari non potest." *Sermo de Aquad.*

[40] under Your protection; reject me not, as I have deserved. Protect me and have pity on me, a miserable sinner. Obtain for me the forgiveness of my sins; obtain for me holy perseverance, the love of God, a good death, and a happy eternity. I hope all things of You, because You are most powerful with God. Make me holy, since You have it in Your power to do so, by Your holy intercession.

Mary! in You do I confide, in You do I place all my hopes, next to Your divine Son Jesus.

MEDITATION 16.
Jesus suffering for our Sins.

1. Seeing men lost in their sins, God was pleased to take pity on them; but his divine justice required satisfaction, and there was no one capable of making adequate satisfaction. On this account he sent into the world his own Son, made man, and loaded him with all our offenses: *The Lord laid on him the iniquity of us all*,[1] so that he might pay our debts, satisfy divine justice, and save mankind.

O eternal God! what more could You have done

to induce us to confide in Your mercy, and to attract our hearts to Your love, than give us even Your own Son? But how could I, after all that You have done for me, have been guilty of so many offenses against You? O my God! for the love of this Your Son, have pity on me.

I am sorry above every evil for having offended You. And though I have grievously offended You, I desire to love You with the greatest fervor; give me strength so to love You.

2. The eternal Father having loaded his Son with all our crimes, was not content even with such satisfaction from him, as would have amply atoned for us all, but, as

1 "Posuit Dominus in eo iniquitatem omnium nostrum." Isaiah 53.6.

[41] Isaiah continues: *The Lord was pleased to bruise him in infirmity.*1 He would have him mangled to exhaustion, with scourges, thorns, nails, and torments, until he died of tortures on an infamous cross.

If faith, O God! did not assure us of this excess of Your love towards men, who could possibly believe it?

God, worthy of all love! permit us not to be any more ungrateful to You. Enlighten and strengthen us to correspond with such immense love during the remainder of our lives; do this, we beseech You, for the love of this Your Son, whom You have given to us.

3. Behold that innocent Son, attentive to the will of his Father, who would have him thus sacrificed for our sins, full of humility before his Father, full of love towards us, obediently embraces his life of pain and his bitter death: *He humbled Himself, becoming obedient unto death, even to the death of the cross.***2**

Dearest Savior, I will therefore say to You with the penitent Ezechiel: *You have delivered my soul that it should not perish; You have cast all my sins behind Your back.***3**

I have deserved by my sins to be cast into hell, but You have delivered me from it, and, as I hope, pardoned me. I have offended Your divine majesty, and You have loaded Yourself with my crimes, and have suffered for me. After this, if I should again offend You, or if I should not love You with my whole heart, what punishment will ever be sufficient for my chastisement? Beloved Jesus, O love of my soul! I am exceedingly sorry for having so grievously offended You. I give You my whole self; receive me, and permit me not to be any-more separated from You. Holy Virgin, Mary, Mother,

1 "Dominus voluit conterere eum in infirmitate." Isaiah 53.10.
2 "Humiliavit semetipsum, factus obediens usque ad mortem, mortem autem crucis." Phil. 2.8.
3 "Tu autem eruisti animam meam, ut non periret; projecisti post tergum tuum omnia peccata mea." Isaiah 38.17.

[42] pray to Your divine Son for me, that he may be

pleased to receive me, and make me all his own.

MEDITATION 17.
The One Thing Necessary.

1. *One thing is necessary***1**: the salvation of our souls. It
is not necessary to be great, noble, or rich in this world,
or to enjoy uninterrupted health; but it is necessary to
save our souls. For this has God placed us here: not to
acquire honors, riches, or pleasures, but to acquire by our
good works that eternal kingdom which is prepared for
those who, during this present life, fight against and
overcome the enemies of their eternal salvation.
Ah, my Jesus, how often have I renounced heaven by
renouncing Your grace! But, O Lord! I am more grieved
for having forfeited Your friendship than for having lost
heaven. Give me, O Jesus! a great sorrow for my sins,
and mercifully pardon me.

2. Of what consequence is it if a man be poor, lowly,
infirm, and despised in this life, provided that in the
end he dies in the grace of God and secures his salvation?
The more he has been afflicted with tribulations, if he
suffered them with patience, the more will he be glori-
fied in the kingdom of heaven. On the other hand,
what does it profit a man to abound in riches and honors,
if, when he dies, he is lost forever? If we are lost, all
the goods that we have enjoyed in this world will be re-

membered only to increase our misery for eternity.

O my God, enlighten me; grant me to understand that my only evil is to offend You, and my only good to love You. Enable me to spend the remainder of my days in serving You.

3. Salvation is necessary, because there is no middle

1 "Unum est necessarium." Luke 10.42.

[43] way - we must either be saved or lost. It will not do to say: I shall be satisfied with not going to hell; I shall not be concerned at being deprived of heaven. No; either heaven or hell; either forever happy with God in heaven in an ocean of delights, or forever trampled upon by devils in hell in an ocean of fire and torments: either saved, or lost; there is no alternative.

Jesus! I have until now chosen hell, and for years past I should have been suffering there, if in pity You had not put up with me. I thank You, O my Savior! and I am sorry above every evil for having offended You. I hope, for the future, with the assistance of Your grace, to walk no more in the way that conducts to hell. I love You, O my sovereign good! and I desire to love You forever. Grant me perseverance in good, and save me through that blood which You have shed for me. O Mary, my hope! intercede for me.

MEDITATION 18.
The Sinner's Disobedience to God.

1. Pharaoh, when Moses announced to him the orders
of God for the liberation of the Hebrews, insolently answered, *Who is the Lord, that I should hear His word?...
I know not the Lord.***1** It is thus that the sinner replies to
his own conscience when it teaches him the divine
precepts, which forbid him to do that which is evil: "I
know not God; I know that he is my Lord, but I will
not obey him."
Thus have I too often addressed You, O God! when
I have committed sin. If you had not died for me,
my Redeemer! I should not dare to crave Your pardon;
but You have offered me Your pardon from the cross, if
I be desirous of availing myself of it. I do indeed desire

1 "Quis est Dominus, ut audiam vocem ejus? . . . Nescio Dominum."
Exod. 5.2.

[44] it; I am sorry for having despised You, my sovereign
good. I will rather die than offend You any more.

2. *You have broken my yoke; you said, I will not serve.***1**
The sinner, when tempted to commit sin, hears indeed
the voice of God, saying to him, "My son, do not revenge Yourself, do not gratify yourself with that sinful
pleasure; relinquish the possession of that which is not
yours." But by yielding to sin, he replies, "Lord, I will
not serve You. You desire that I should not commit this

sin, but I will commit it."

My Lord and my God, how frequently have I, not by
my words, but my deeds and my will, thus daringly replied to You! Alas! *cast me not away from Your face.*2
I am now sensible of the wrong I have done You in
parting with Your graces for the gratification of my own
wretched desires. Oh that I had died rather than ever
offended You!

3. God is the Lord of all things, because he has created
all. *All things are in Your power, because You have
made heaven and earth, and all things that are under
the heavens.*3 All creatures obey God; the heavens,
the earth, the sea, the elements, the lower creatures; while
man, although he has been gifted and loved by God
above all other creatures, obeys him not, and is heedless
of the loss of his grace!

I give You thanks, O God, for having waited for me.
What would have become of me, had I died in one of
those nights in which I went to rest under Your displease-
ure? But as You have patiently waited for me, it is a
sign that You are desirous of pardoning me. Pardon
me then, O Jesus! I am sorry above every evil for

1 "Confregisti jugum meum . . . et dixisti: Non serviam," Jer. 2.20.
2 "Ne projicias me a facie tua." Ps. 1.13.
3 "In ditione enim tua cuncta sunt posita, et non est qui possit tuae
resistere voluntati." Esther 13.9.

[45] having ever lost the respect which is due to You. But then I did not love You; now I do love You more than myself, and I am ready to die a thousand times rather than again forfeit Your grace and friendship. You have said that You love those who love You.**1** I love You; do love me in return, and give me grace to live and die in Your love; that so I may love You forever. Mary, my refuge, through You do I hope to remain faithful to God until the hour of my death.

MEDITATION 19.
The Merciful Chastisements of God.

1. God, being infinite goodness, desires only our good and to communicate to us his own happiness. When he chastises us, it is because we have obliged him to do so by our sins. Hence the prophet Isaiah says that on such occasions he does a work foreign to his desires.**2** Hence it is said that it is the property of God to have mercy and to spare, to dispense his favors and to make all happy.

God! it is this Your infinite goodness which sinners offend and despise, when they provoke You to chastise them. Wretch that I am, how often have I offended Your infinite goodness!

2. Let us therefore understand that when God threatens us it is not because he desires to punish us, but because

he wishes to deliver us from punishment; he threatens because he would have compassion on us. *O God, . . . You have been angry, and have had mercy on us.***3** But how is this? he is angry with us, and treats us with mercy? Yes! He shows himself angry towards us, in order that we may amend our lives, and that thus he may be able

1 "Ego diligentes me diligo." Prov. 13.17.
2 "Alienum opus ejus . . . peregrinum est opus ejus ab eo." Isaiah 28.21.
3 "Deus, . . . iratus es, et misertus es nobis." Ps. 59.3.

[46] to pardon and save us; from here if in this life he chastises us for our sins, he does so in his mercy, for by so doing he frees us from eternal woe. How unfortunate, then, is the sinner who escapes punishment in this life!

Since then, O God! I have so much offended You, chastise me in this life, that You may spare me in the next. I know that I have certainly deserved hell; I accept all kinds of pain, that You may reinstate me in Your grace and deliver me from hell, where I should be forever separated from You. Enlighten and strengthen me to overcome every obstacle to Your favor.

3. He who makes no account of the divine threats ought to fear much lest the chastisement threatened in the Proverbs should suddenly overtake him. The man that with a stiff neck despises him that reproves him, shall suddenly be destroyed; and health shall not follow him.**1** A sudden death shall overtake him that despises God's war-

nings, and he shall have no time to avoid eternal destruction.

This, O Jesus! has happened to many, and I indeed have deserved that the same should happen to me; but,

my Redeemer! You have shown that mercy towards me which You have not shown to many others who have offended You less frequently than I have done, and who are now suffering in hell without the least hope of ever again being able to regain Your favor. I know, O Lord! that You desire my salvation, and I also desire it, that I may please You. I renounce all, and turn myself to You, who are my God and my only good. I believe in You, I hope in You, I love You, and You alone. O infinite goodness! I am exceedingly displeased with myself for having until now done evil against You; and I wish that I had suffered every evil rather than offended You. Do not allow me any more to depart from You,

1 "Viro qui corripientem dura cervice contemnit, repentinus ei superveniet interitus, et eum sanitas non sequetur." Prov. 29.1.

[47] rather let me die than offer You so great an injury. In You, my crucified Jesus, do I place all my hopes. O Mary, mother of Jesus! recommend me to Your Son.

MEDITATION 20.
The Patience of God with Sinners.

1. The more we have experienced the patient mercies
of God, the more we ought to be afraid of continuing to
abuse them, lest the time of God's vengeance overtake
us. *Revenge is Mine, and I will repay in due time.* **1** God
will put an end to his forbearance towards those who
will not cease to abuse it.

I give You thanks, O Lord! for having patiently
borne with me, though I have so often betrayed You.
Make me sensible of the evil that I have done by abusing Your patience for so long a time; make me sorry for
all the offenses I have committed against You. No, I
will never more abuse Your tender mercy.

2. "Commit this sin; you can afterwards confess it."
Such is the deceit with which the devil has drawn
many souls into hell. Many Christians, now in hell,
have been lost by this delusion. *The Lord waits, that
He may have mercy on you.* **2** God waits for the sinner,
that the sinner may be converted, and obtain mercy;
but when God sees that the time which he allows the
sinner for doing penance is employed only in increasing
the number of his offenses, then he waits no longer, but
punishes him as he deserves.

Pardon me, O God! for I desire never more to offend

You. And why should I delay? that You may condemn
me to hell? I fear indeed that now You can no longer
have patience with me. I have indeed offended You
too grievously. I am sorry for it. I repent of it.

1 "Mea est ultio, et ego retribuam in tempore." Deut. 32.35.
2 "Exspectat Dominus, ut misereatur vestri." Isaiah 30.18.

[48] I hope for forgiveness through the merits of that
blood which You have shed for me.

3. It is the mercies of the Lord that we are not consumed: *because His mercies have not failed.***1** Thus
should he exclaim who finds, to his confusion, that he
has frequently offended God. He should be most grateful to God for not having permitted him to die in his sins,
and be most careful not to offend him again; otherwise
the Lord will reproach him, saying: *What more could I
have done for My vineyard that I have not done?***2** God
will say to him: Ungrateful soul! If you had committed
the same offenses against man, who is viler than the
earth, truly he would not have borne with you. And
how great mercies have I exercised towards you! How
many times have I called you, and enlightened you,
and pardoned you? The time of punishment is at
hand; the time of forgiveness is past. Thus has God
spoken to many who are now suffering in hell; where
one of their greatest torments is the remembrance of
the mercies which they formerly received from God.

Jesus, my Redeemer and my Judge! I also have deserved to hear the same from Your mouth; but I hear You now again calling me to pardon: *Be converted to the Lord Your God*:3 O accursed sin, which has made me lose my God, how much do I abhor and detest You! I turn my whole self towards You, my Lord and my God! My sovereign good, I love You; and because I love You I repent with my whole soul for having, during the time that is past, so much despised You. My God! I desire never more to offend You: give me Your love, grant me perseverance. Mary, my refuge, attend to and help me.

1 "Misericordise Domini, quia non sumus consumpti." Lam. 3.22.
2 "Quid est quod debui ultra facere vineae mese et non feci? Isaiah 5.4.
3 "Convertere ad Dominum Deum tuum." Hosea 14.2.

MEDITATION 21.
Death, the Passage to Eternity.

[49] 1. It is an article of faith that my soul is immortal, and that one day, when I least think of it, I must leave this world. I ought therefore to make a provision for myself, which will not fail with this life, but will be eternal even as I am eternal. Great things were done here, in their life time, by an Alexander or a Caesar; but for how many ages past have their glories ceased! and where are they now?

O my God, that I had always loved You! What now remains for me, after so many years spent in sin, but trouble and remorse of conscience? But since You allow me time to repair the evil which I have done, behold me, Lord, ready to perform whatever You require of me, whatever You please. I will spend the remainder of my days in bewailing my ungrateful conduct towards You, and in loving You with all my power, my God and my all, my only good.

2. What will it avail me to have been happy in this world (if indeed true happiness can be attained without God) if hereafter I should be miserable for all eternity? But what folly it is, to know that I must die, and that an eternity either of happiness or misery awaits me after death, and that upon dying badly or well depends my being miserable or happy forever, and yet, not to adopt every means in my power to secure a good death!

Holy Spirit, enlighten and strengthen me to live always in Your grace, until the hour of my departure. O infinite goodness! I am sensible of the evil which I have done by offending You, and I detest it: I know that You alone are worthy of being loved, and I love You above all things.

3. In a word, all the good things of this life must end [50] at our burial and be left, while we are mouldering in our graves. The shadow of death will cover and obscure

all the grandeur and splendor of this world. He only, then, can be called happy who serves God in this world, and by loving and serving him acquires eternal happiness.

O Jesus! I am truly sorry for having until now made so little account of Your love. Now I love You above all things, and I desire nothing else but to love You. Henceforth You only shall be the sole object of my love, You only shall be my all; and this is the only inheritance I ask of You; to love You always, both in this life and in the next. For the merits of Your bitter Passion, give me perseverance in all virtues. Mary, mother of God, You are my hope.

MEDITATION 22.
The Reformation of our Lives before Death.

1. Every one desires to die the death of the saints, but it is scarcely possible for the Christian to make a holy end who has led a disorderly life until the time of his death; to die united with God, after having always lived at a distance from him. The saints, in order to secure a happy death, renounced all the riches, the delights, and all the hopes which this world held out to them, and embraced poor and mortified lives. They buried themselves alive in this world, to avoid, when dead, being buried forever in hell.

O God! for how many years past have I deserved to be buried in that place of torments, without hope of pardon, or of being able to love You! But You have waited in order to pardon me. Truly, then, am I sorry from the bottom of my heart for having offended You, my sovereign good; and have pity on me, and do not permit me to offend You any more.

[51] 2. God forewarns sinners that they will seek him in death and will not find him: *You shall seek and shall not find Me.***1** They shall not find him because they will not then seek him through love, but only through the fear of hell; they will seek God without renouncing their affection for sin, and from here they shall not find him.

No, my God, I will not wait to seek You in death, but will seek and desire You from this moment. I am sorry for having until now given You so much displeasure by seeking to gratify my own inclinations. I am sorry for it, I confess that I have done evil. But You do not will that the heart that seeks You should despair, but rejoice: *Let the heart of them rejoice that seek the Lord.***2** Yes, O Lord! I seek You, and I love You more than myself.

3. How miserable is the Christian who before his death has not spent a good part of his life in bewailing his sins! It is not to be denied that such a man may be converted at his death and obtain salvation; but the

mind obscured, the heart hardened, the bad habits formed, the passions predominant, render it morally impossible for him to die happily. An extraordinary grace will be necessary for him; but does God reserve such a grace to bestow it upon one who has continued ungrateful to him even until the moment of death? O God, to what straits are sinners reduced to escape eternal destruction!

No, my God, I will not wait until death to repent of my sins and to love You. I am sorry now for having offended You; now do I love You with my whole heart. Do not allow me any more to turn my back upon You; rather let me die. O holy Mother, Mary, obtain for me perseverance in virtue.

1 "Quaeretis me, et non invenietis." John 7.34.
2 "Laetetur cor quaerentium Dominum." Ps. 104.3.

MEDITATION 23.
The Lamb of God Sacrificed for our Sins.

[52] 1. *Behold the Lamb of God*;**1** thus did the Baptist speak of our Blessed Redeemer, who offered his blood and even his life in sacrifice to obtain our pardon and our eternal salvation. Behold him in the hall of Pilate; as an innocent Lamb he permits himself to be shorn, not of wool, but of his sacred flesh, with thorns and scourges. *He shall be dumb as a lamb before His shearer, and He*

*shall not open His mouth.***2** He opens not his mouth, nor does he complain, because he desires to suffer himself the punishments due to our sins.

May the angels and all creatures bless You, O Savior of the world! for the great mercy and love which You have shown towards us. We have committed sins, and You did make satisfaction for them.

2. Behold him, bound like a malefactor and surrounded by executioners, conducted to Calvary, there to become the victim of the great sacrifice, by which the work of our redemption is to be accomplished: *I was as a meek lamb that is carried to be a victim.***3**

To where, O Jesus! do the people conduct You, loaded with such a cross, after having so cruelly tormented You? You answer me: They conduct Me to death, and I go willingly, because I am going to save you, and to prove how great my love is towards you. And how, O my Savior! have I proved my love towards You? You indeed know: by injuries and grievous offenses, and by my frequent contempt of Your grace and love.

1 "Ecce Agnus Dei." John 1.29.
2 "Quasi agnus coram tondente se, obmutescet, et non aperiet os suum." Isaiah 53.7.
3 "Et ego quasi agnus mansuetus, qui portatur ad victimam." Jer. 11.19.

[53] But Your death is my hope. I am sorry, O love of

my soul! for having offended You; I am sorry, and will love You with my whole heart.

3. St. Francis of Assisi, seeing a lamb led to the slaughter, could not refrain from tears, saying, "As this lamb is led to the slaughter, so was my innocent Lord conducted for me to the death of the cross."

Since, then, O Jesus! You do not refuse to go to sacrifice Your life for the love of me, shall I refuse to give my whole self for the love of You? This You require of me: *You shall love the Lord Your God.*1 This, and this only, do I desire - to love You, and to love You with my whole heart. You have loved without any reserve, and so will I love You. I am sorry for having offended You, O Lamb of God! and I give my whole self to You. Receive me, O Jesus! and make me faithful to Your grace. O Mary, Mother of my Redeemer, make me by Your prayers entirely his!

MEDITATION 24.
The Value of Time.

1. Time is a treasure of inestimable value, because in every moment of time we may gain an increase of grace and eternal glory. In hell the lost souls are tormented with the thought, and bitterly lament that now there is no more time for them in which to rescue themselves by

repentance from eternal misery. What would they give but for one hour of time to save themselves by an act of true sorrow from destruction! In heaven there is no grief; but if the blessed could grieve, they would do so for having lost so much time during life, in which they might have acquired greater glory, and because time is now no longer theirs.

1 "Diliges Dominum Deum tuum." Matt. 22.37.
[54] I give You thanks, O God! for giving me time to bewail my sins, and to make amends by my love for the offenses I have committed against You.

2. Nothing is so precious as time; and yet how is it that nothing is so little valued? Men will spend hours in jesting, or standing at a window or in the middle of a road, to see what passes; and if you ask them what they are doing, they will tell you they are passing away time. O time, now so much despised! You will be of all things else the most valued by such persons when death shall have surprised them. What will they not then be willing to give for one hour of so much lost time! But time will remain no longer for them when it is said to each one of them: "Go forth, Christian soul, out of this world:" I hasten to be gone, for now there is no time for You. How will they then exclaim, lamenting, Alas! I have squandered away my whole life; during so many years I might have become a saint; but how far am I from being such; and shall I become such, now that

there is no more time for me?! But to what purpose will such lamentations be, when the dying man is on the verge of that moment on which will depend eternity?

3. *Walk while you have light.***2** The time of death is the time of night, when nothing can any longer be seen, nor anything be accomplished. *The night comes, in which no man can work.***3** Hence the Holy Spirit admonishes us to walk in the way of the Lord, while we have the light and the day before us. Can we reflect that the time is near approaching in which the cause of our eternal salvation is to be decided, and still squander away time? Let us not delay, but immediately put our accounts in order, because when we least think of it, Jesus Christ will come

1 Proficiscere, anima Christiana, de hoc mundo.
2 "Ambulate dum lucem habetis." John 12.35
3 "Venit nox, quando nemo potest operari." John 9.4.

[55] to judge us. *At what hour you think not, the Son of man will come.***1**

Hasten, then, my Jesus, hasten to pardon me. And shall I delay? shall I delay until I am cast into that eternal prison, where, with the rest of the condemned souls, I must forever lament, saying, *The summer is past, and we are not saved.***2** No, my Lord, I will no longer resist Your loving invitations. Who knows but that this meditation which I am now reading may be the last I shall ever cast my eyes upon! I am sorry for having

offended You, O sovereign good! To You do I conse-
crate the remainder of my days, and beseech You to
grant me holy perseverance. I desire never more to
offend You, but forever to love You. O Mary, refuge
of sinners! in You do I place my confidence.

MEDITATION 25.
The Terrors of the Dying Man at the Thought of Approaching Judgment.

1. Consider the fear which the thought of judgment
will cause in the mind of a dying man, when he reflects
that in a very short time he must present himself before
Jesus Christ, his Judge, to render an account of all the
actions of his past life. When the awful moment of his
passage out of this world into another, out of time into
eternity, arrives, then will there be nothing so tormenting to him as the sight of his sins. St. Mary Magdalene
de Pazzi, being ill, and thinking of judgment, trembled.
Her confessor told her not to fear. "Ah, Father," she
replied, "it is an awful thing to appear before Jesus
Christ as our Judge." Such were the sensations of this
holy virgin, who was a saint from her infancy. What
will he say who has frequently deserved hell?

1 "Qua hora non putatis, Filius hominis veniet." Luke 12.40.
2 "Finita est aestas, et nos salvati non sumus." Jer. 8.20.

[56] 2. The abbot Agatho after many years of penance trembled, saying, "What will become of me when I shall be judged?" And how should he not tremble who has offended God by many mortal sins, and yet has done no penance for them? At death, the sight of his crimes, the rigor of the divine judgments, the uncertainty of the sentence to be pronounced upon him, what a tempest of horror and confusion will these raise around him! Let us be careful to throw ourselves at the feet of Jesus Christ, and secure our pardon before the arrival of our accounting day.

Ah! my Jesus and my Redeemer, who will one day be my judge, have pity on me before the day of justice. Behold at Your feet a deserter, who has often promised to be faithful to You, and has as often again turned his back upon You. No, my God, You have not deserved the treatment which You have until now received at my hands. Forgive me, O Lord! for I desire truly to change and amend my life. I am sorry, my sovereign good! for having despised You: take pity on me.

3. Then will be decided the great affair of our eternal salvation. Upon this decision will depend our being either saved or lost forever, our being happy or miserable for all eternity. But, O God! each one knows this, and says, "So it is." But if it is so, why do we not leave all to attend only to our sanctification, and to the securing of our eternal salvation?

My God, I give You thanks for the light which You have given me. Remember, O Jesus! that You did die for my salvation; grant that when I first behold You I may see You appeased. If until now I have despised Your grace, I now esteem it above every other good. I love You, O infinite goodness! and because I love You, I am sorry for having offended You. Until now I have forsaken You, but now I desire You and seek You; grant that I may find You, O God of my soul! Mary, my mother, recommend me to Your Son Jesus.

MEDITATION 26.
The Fire of Hell.

[57] 1. It is certain that hell is a pit of fire, in which the miserable souls of the wicked will be tormented forever. Even in this life the pain of burning is of all pains the most intense and dreadful; but the fire of hell has the power of inflicting much more excruciating torment, because it has been created by God to be the instrument of his wrath upon his rebellious creatures. "*Go, you cursed, into everlasting fire,*" is the sentence of the reprobate. And as in this sentence of condemnation fire is particularly mentioned, we may conclude that, of all the torments with which the senses of the wicked are afflicted, fire is the greatest.

Ah, my God, for how many years past have I deserved

to burn in this fire! But You have waited for me, to behold me burning, not with this dreadful fire, but with the blessed flames of Your holy love. This is how I love You, my sovereign good, and desire to love You forever.

2. In this world fire burns only outwardly, and does not penetrate our interior; but in hell the fire enters into the inmost recesses of its victims. *You shall make them as an oven of fire.***1** Every one will become as a furnace of fire, so that the heart will burn within the chest, the bowels within the belly, the brains within the skull, and even the marrow within the bones. Sinners, what are your feelings with regard to this fire? You, who cannot now bear a spark accidentally fallen from a candle, nor a house too hot, nor a ray of the sun upon your head, how will you endure to be permanently immersed in an ocean of fire, where you will be forever dying, and yet never, never die?

1 "Pones eos ut clibanum ignis." Ps. 20.10.

[58] O my Redeemer! let not that blood which You did shed for the love of me, be shed for me in vain. Grant me sorrow for my sins, grant me Your holy love.

3. *Which of you*, says the prophet, *can dwell with devouring fire?***1** As a wild beast devours his prey, so shall the fire of hell continually devour the unhappy

soul, but without ever depriving him of life. Hence St. Peter Damian exclaims, "Go on, sinner, go on, unchaste one; give Your flesh its desires: a day will come when Your impurities will be to You as pitch within Your bowels, to nourish the fire which will consume You in hell for all eternity."**2**

My God, whom I have despised and lost! forgive me, and permit me not to lose You any more. I am sorry above every evil for having offended You. Receive me into Your favor, for now do I promise You that I will love You, and love no other but You. Most holy Mary, deliver me by Your holy intercession, from ever suffering the torments of hell.

MEDITATION 27.
The Vanity of all Worldly Things.

1. What is life but a vapor, which appears for a short time and then is seen no more? *What is your life?* says St. James. *It is a vapor which appear s for a little while, and afterwards shall vanish away.***3** The vapors which arise from the earth, when raised into the air and surrounded by the rays of the sun, appear brilliant and beautiful; but the least wind disperses them, and they

---

1 "Quis poterit habitare de vobis cum igne devorante?" Isaiah 33.14.
2 "Libido tua vertetur in picem, qua se perpetuus ignis in tuis visceribus nutriat." *Opusc. de cael. Sac.*, ch. 3.
3 "Quid est enim vita vestra? vapor est ad modicum parens, et

deinceps exterminabitur." James 4.15.

[59] are seen no more. Such is the grandeur of this world. Behold that prince; today, he is feared, attended upon and honored by thousands; tomorrow, he will be dead, despised and hated by all. In a word, honors, pleasures, and riches must all end in death.

my God! make me sensible of the immensity of Your goodness, that I may love nothing but You.

2. Death deprives man of whatever he may possess in this world. What a sad sight, to behold a rich man, after death, carried out of his palace, to return there no more! How sad to behold others taking possession of the estates which he has left, of his wealth, and whatever else he so lately enjoyed! His servants, after having accompanied him to his grave, abandon him, and leave him there, to be devoured by worms; no one esteeming him, no one flattering him. Formerly every one obeyed his nod, but now no one takes the least notice of his orders.

How wretched have I been, O Lord! in having, for so many years, gone after the vanities of the world, and left You, my sovereign good! But from this day forward I desire to possess You as my only treasure, as the only love of my soul.

3. *Dust and ashes, why are you proud?***1** Man, says the Almighty, do you not see that in a short time you will become dust and ashes? and on what do you fix your thoughts and affections? Reflect that death will soon rob You of everything, and separate You from the whole world. And if, when You give in your accounts, you be found lacking, what will become of you for eternity?

I give You thanks, my Lord and my God. You speak thus to me, because You desire to save me. Let Your mercies now prevail. You have promised to pardon such as repent of their offenses against You.

1 "Quid superbit terra et cinis?" Eccles. 10.9.

[60] From the bottom of my heart I repent: grant me therefore pardon. You have promised to love those who love You: above all things do I now love You; and so do love me also, and hate me not any more, as I have deserved. O Mary, my advocate, in Your protection is my hope.

MEDITATION 28.
The Number of our Sins.

1. It is the opinion of St. Basil, St. Jerome, St. Amorose, St. Augustine, and others, that as God has determined for each one the number of talents, the goods of fortune, and the number of days to be bestowed upon

him, so he has also determined for each one the number of sins to be pardoned him, which being completed, God will pour out his chastisements upon him and pardon him no more. *Each one,* says St. Augustine, *is patiently borne with by Almighty God for a certain time; but when this is over, there is then no longer any more pardon for him.***1**

I am aware, O God! that I have until now abused Your patience too much; but I know that You have not yet abandoned me, because I am sorry for my sins, and this sorrow is a sign that You still love me. O my God! I desire never more to displease You; for pity's sake do not abandon me.

2. *The Lord patiently expects that when the day of judgment shall come, He may punish them in the fullness of their sins.***2** Although God has patience and waits for the sinner, yet, when the day arrives for the measure of his

1 "Tamdiu unumquemque a Dei patientia sustentari, quamdiu nondum finem repleverit; quo consummate, nullam illi veniam reservari."
De Vita Christi, ch. 3.
2 "Dominus patienter exspectat, ut eas (nationes), cum judicii dies advenerit, in plenitudine peccatorum puniat." 2 Mach. 6.14.

[61] sins to be filled up he will wait for him no longer, but chastise him.

O Lord! wait yet for me a little while, do not yet abandon me; I hope with the assistance of Your grace never to offend You more, nor to excite Your anger against me. I am sorry, O my sovereign good! for having offended You, and I protest that I will never more betray You. I now esteem Your friendship more than all the goods of the whole world.

3. We commit sins, and we take no notice of the load of guilt which we are accumulating; but let us tremble lest what happened to King Balthasar befall us also: *You are weighed in the balance, and are found wanting.*[1] The devil may tell you that it matters not whether it be ten or eleven sins. But no, that wicked enemy deceives you; the sin which he is tempting you to commit will increase the load of your guilt; it may decide the balance of divine justice against you, and you may be condemned for it to the torments of hell. If, O Christian, you live not in fear that God will not show you mercy, should you add one more mortal sin to those which you have already committed; if you tremble not at the thought of this, you are in great danger of being lost.

No, my God: You have borne with me too long; I will never more abuse Your bountiful goodness. I thank You for having waited for me until now. I have forfeited Your love too often; but I hope never more to lose You. Since You have not yet abandoned me, enable me to find You again. I love You, O my God! and I am sorry from the bottom of my heart for having ever turned my back upon You. No, I desire never more to lose You. Assist me with Your grace. And You, my

queen and my mother, Mary, help me by Your holy
intercession.

1. "Appensus es in statera, et inventus es minus habens." Dan. 5.27.

MEDITATION 29.
The Folly of Living as Enemies of God.

[62] 1. Sinners call the saints who, in this life, fly from
honors, riches, and the pleasures of sense, and embrace
poverty, contempt, and mortification, fools. But at the
day of final retribution they will confess that they themselves have been fools in judging the lives of the saints to
be folly: *We fools esteemed their life madness.***1** And what
greater folly can there be than to live without God? which
is to live a miserable life in this world, to be succeeded
by a still more miserable one in hell.

No, I will not wait till the last day to confess my folly;
I now confess it: how great has it been in offending
You, my sovereign good! *Father, I am not worthy to
be called your son.***2** Father, I am not worthy to receive
Your forgiveness, but I hope for it through the blood
which You have shed for my sake. My Jesus, I am
sorry for having despised You, I love You above all
things.

2. Unhappy sinners! blinded by their sins, they lose
all judgment. What would be said of a man who should

sell a kingdom for the smallest coin? And what should
be said of him who, for a momentary pleasure, a vapor,
a caprice, sells heaven and the grace of God? They
think only of this life, which will shortly end, and in the
meantime deserve hell for that life which will never
end. O my God! permit me not to become any more
so blind as to prefer, as I have until now done, my own
unlawful gratifications before You, and for the sake
of them to despise You, my sovereign good! I now
detest them, and love You above all things.

1 "Nos insensati vitam illorum aestimabamus insaniam." Wis. 5.4.
2 "Pater . . . non sum dignus vocari filius tuus." Luke 15.19.

[63] 3. Miserable worldlings! the time will come when
they will bewail their folly; but when? when there will
be no longer anything to prevent their eternal ruin.
Then will they say, *What has pride profited us? or what
advantage has the boasting of riches brought us? All those
things are passed away like a shadow.***1** Behold, they will
exclaim, how all our delights have passed away like a
shadow, and nothing remains to us now but suffering
and eternal lamentation!

Dear Jesus! have pity on me. I have forgotten You,
but You did not forget me. I love You with my
whole soul, and I detest above all evil whatever sins I
have committed against You. Pardon me, O God! and
remember not my offenses against You. And since

You know my weakness, do not abandon me; give me strength to overcome all things to please You. O Mary, Mother of God! in You do I place my hopes.

MEDITATION 30.
The Sacred Wounds of Jesus.

1. St. Bonaventure says that the wounds of Jesus wound the hardest hearts and inflame the coldest souls.[2] And in truth, how can we believe that God permitted himself to be struck, scourged, crowned with thorns, and finally put to death for the love of us, and yet not love him? St. Francis of Assisi frequently bewailed the ingratitude of men as he passed along the country, saying, "Love is not loved, love is not loved ."

Behold, O my Jesus! I am one of those who are thus ungrateful, who have been so many years in the world and have not loved You. And shall I, my Redeemer,

1 "Quid nobis profuit superbia? aut divitiarum jactantia quid contulit nobis? Transierunt omnia illa tanquam umbra." Wis. 5.8.
2 "Vulnera corda saxea vulnerantia, et mentes congelatas inflammantia." *Stim. div. am.,* Pt. 1, ch. 1.

[64] remain forever such? No, I will love You until death, and will give myself wholly to You; mercifully accept me and help me.

2. The Church, when she shows us Jesus Christ crucified, exclaims: *"His whole figure breathes forth love;
his head bowed down, his arms extended, his side
opened."***1** She cries out: Behold, O man! behold Your
God, who has died for Your love; see how his arms are
extended to embrace You, his head bowed down to give
You the kiss of peace, his side opened to give You access
to his heart, if You will but love him.

Assuredly I will love You, my treasure, my love, and
my all. And whom shall I love, if I love not God who
has died for me?

3. *The love of Christ,* says the Apostle, *urges us.***2**
Ah! my Redeemer, You have died for the love of men;
yet men do not love You, because they live unmindful of
the death which You have suffered for them. If only they
bore it in mind, how could they live without loving You?
"Knowing," says St. Francis de Sales, "that Jesus being
really God, has so loved us as to suffer the death of
the cross for us, do we not on this account feel our
hearts, as it were, in a press, in which they are forcibly
held, and love expressed from them by a kind of violence,
which is the more powerful as it is the more amiable?"
And this is what St. Paul says in these words: *The love
of Christ urges us;***3** the love of Jesus Christ forces us to
love him.

Ah! my beloved Savior, heretofore I have despised

You, but now I esteem and love You more than my own life; nothing afflicts me so much as the remem-

1 "Omnis figura ejus amorem spirat, et ad redamandum provocat, caput inclinatum, manus expansae, pectus apertum. *Off. Dolor. B. V.* resp. 1.
2 "Charitas Christi urget nos." 2 Cor. 5.14.
3 Charitas Christi urget nos.

[65] brance of the many offenses I have committed against You. Pardon me, O Jesus! and draw my whole heart to Yourself, that so I may not desire, nor seek, nor sigh after any other beside You. O Mary, my mother! help me to love Jesus.

MEDITATION 31.
The Great Affair of Salvation.

1. The affair of our eternal salvation is of all affairs the most important. But how does it happen that men use all diligence to succeed in the affairs of this world, leave no means untried to obtain a desirable situation, to gain a lawsuit, or to bring about a marriage, reject no counsels, neglect no measures by which to obtain their object, going without food and sleep, and yet do nothing to gain eternal salvation, nothing to gain it, but everything to forfeit it, as though hell, heaven, and eternity were not articles of faith, but only fables and lies?

O God! assist me by Your divine light; permit me not to be any longer blinded, as I until now have been.

2. If an accident happen to a house, what is not immediately done to repair it? If a jewel be lost, what is not done to recover it? The soul is lost, the grace of God is lost, and men sleep and smile We attend most carefully to our temporal welfare, and almost entirely neglect our eternal salvation! We call those happy who have renounced all things for God; why then are we so much attached to earthly things?

O Jesus! You have so much desired my salvation as to shed Your blood and lay down Your life to secure it; and I have been so indifferent to the preservation of Your grace as to renounce and forfeit it for a mere nothing! I am sorry, O Lord! for having thus dishonored You. I will renounce all things to attend only to Your love, my God, who are most worthy of all love.

[66] 3. The Son of God gives his life to save our souls; the devil is most diligent in his endeavors to bring them to eternal ruin: and do we take no care of them? St. Philip Neri convicts that man of the height of folly who is inattentive to the salvation of his soul. Let us arouse our faith: it is certain that, after this short life, another life awaits us, which will be either eternally happy or eternally miserable. God has given us to choose which we will. *Before man is life and death . . . that which he*

*shall choose shall be given him.***1** Ah! let us make such a choice now as we shall not have to repent of for all eternity.

God! make me sensible of the great wrong I have done You in offending You and renouncing You for the love of creatures. I am sorry with my whole heart for having despised You, my sovereign good; do not reject me now that I return to You. I love You above all things, and for the future I will lose all things rather than forfeit Your grace. Through the love which You have shown me in dying for me, attend to me with Your help, and do not abandon me. O Mary, Mother of God! be my advocate.

MEDITATION 32.
The Frequent thought of Death.

1. Men who are attached to this world endeavor to banish the thoughts of death from their minds, as though, by avoiding the remembrance of death, they could avoid death itself. But no; by banishing the thoughts of death from their minds, they expose themselves to greater danger of making an evil end. There is no alternative: sooner or later we must die; and what is still more, we can die but once; and if once we lost, we shall be lost forever.

1 "Ante hominem vita et mors, bonum et malum; quod placuerit ei,

dabitur illi." Eccles. 15.18.

[67] My God, I give You thanks for having enlightened
me. I have already lost too many years in offending You;
but I will now spend the remainder of my life entirely in
Your service. Command me what You will, for I desire
to please You in all things.

2. Holy anchorites, who formerly fled from the world
into deserts in order to secure for themselves a happy
death, took nothing with them but some spiritual book
and a skull, by the sight of which they might continually
keep up in their minds the remembrance of their last
end. They meditated upon it, saying: "As the bones
of him to whom this skull belonged, so will the bones of
my body one day be: and my soul - who knows where
that shall dwell?" And thus they endeavored to gain
not the goods of this life, but of that life which will
never end.

I give You thanks, O Lord! for not having permitted me
to die when I was in the state of sin. I am sorry for having
offended You, and hope, through Your precious blood,
for mercy and pardon. I desire, O Jesus! to renounce all
things, and to do my utmost to please You.

3. A certain hermit, being at the point of death, was ob-
served to smile, and being asked why he was so cheerful,
answered: "I have always kept death before my eyes, and

from here, now that it has come, it does not alarm me."
The approach of death, therefore, is terrible to those only
who have thought of nothing but of gratifying themselves
during their lifetime, and have never thought of their last
end; but it is not terrible to those who, by frequently
thinking upon it, have learned to despise all earthly
goods, and to love nothing but God.

O my Savior! I perceive that death is already drawing
near to me, and as yet I have done nothing for You,
who did die for me. No, before death, I will, O God!
love You, who are worthy of infinite love. I [68] have
until now dishonored You by the offenses which I
have committed against You; but I am sorry for them
with my whole heart. For the future I will honor You,
by loving You to the utmost of my power. Give me
light and strength to do so. You would have me be
wholly Yours, and such do I desire to be. Help me by
Your grace; in You do I confide. And in You also do
I confide, O Mary, my Mother, and my hope!

MEDITATION 33.
The Turning away from God by Sin.

1. St. Augustine and St. Thomas define mortal sin to
be a turning away from God : that is, the turning of one's
back upon God, leaving the Creator for the sake of the
creature. What punishment would that subject deserve

who, while his king was giving him a command, contemptuously turned his back upon him to go and transgress his orders? This is what the sinner does; and this is punished in hell with the pain of loss, that is, the loss of God, a punishment richly deserved by him who in this life turns his back upon his sovereign good. Alas! my God, I have frequently turned my back upon You; but I see that You have not yet abandoned me; I see that You approach me, and inviting me to repentance, offer me Your pardon. I am sorry above every evil for having offended You, have pity on me.

2. *You have forsaken Me, says the Lord, You have gone backward.***1** God complains and says, Ungrateful soul, you have forsaken me! I should never have forsaken you had you not first turned your back upon Me: *you have gone backward***2** - O God, with what consternation

1 "Tu reliquisti me, dicit Dominus; retrorsum abiisti." Jer. 15.6.
2 Retrorsum abiisti.

[69] will these words fill the soul of the sinner when he stands to be judged before Your divine tribunal!

You make me hear them now, O my Savior! not to condemn me, but to bring me to sorrow for the offenses I have committed against You. Yes, O Jesus! I sincerely repent of all the displeasure which I have given You. For my own miserable gratifications I have forsaken You, my God, my sovereign, infinite good! But behold me a penitent returned to You; and reject me not.

3. *Why will you die, O house of Israel? return and live.***1** I have died, says Jesus Christ, for the salvation of your souls, and why will you condemn them by your sins to eternal death? Return to me, and you will recover the life of my grace.

Jesus! I should not dare to crave Your pardon, did I not know that You had died to obtain my forgiveness. Alas! how often have I despised Your grace and Your love! O that I had died rather than ever offered You so great an injury! But You, who came near to me even when I offended You, will not now reject me, when I love You and seek no other but You. My God and my all, permit me not any more to be ungrateful to You. Mary, Queen and Mother, obtain for me the grace of holy perseverance.

MEDITATION 34.
The Mercy of God in Calling Sinners to Repentance.

1. The Lord called to Adam, and said to him, *Where are You?***2** These are the words of a father, says a pious author, going in quest of his lost son. Oh the immense compassion of our God! Adam sins, he turns his back

[70] upon God; and yet God does not abandon him, but
follows him and calls after him, "Adam, where are You?"
Thus, my soul, has God frequently done towards you;
you have forsaken him by sin; but he did not hesitate
to approach you, and to call upon you by many interior
lights, by remorse of conscience, and by his holy inspirations; all of which were the effects of his compassion
and love.

God of mercy, O God of love! how could I have so
grievously offended You, how could I have been so ungrateful to You!

2. As a father when he beholds his son hastening to
cast himself down from the brink of a precipice, presses
forward towards him, and with tears endeavors to withhold him from destruction; so, my God, have You done
towards me. I was already hastening by my sins to
precipitate myself into hell, and You did hold me
back. I am now sensible, O Lord! of the love which
You have shown me, and I hope to sing forever in
heaven the praises of Your mercy: *The mercies of the
Lord I will sing forever.*1 I know, O Jesus! that You desire
my salvation; but I do not know whether You have yet
pardoned me. Oh! give me intense sorrow for my sins,
give me an ardent love for You, as signs of Your merci-

ful forgiveness.

3. O my Savior! how can I doubt of receiving Your
pardon, when You Yourself do offer it to me, and are
ready to receive me with open arms on my return to
You? And so I do return to You, sorrowing and
overpowered at the consideration that after all my
offenses against You, You indeed still love me. Oh
that I had never displeased You, my sovereign good!
how much am I grieved for having done so! Pardon me,
O Jesus! I will never more offend You. But I shall not

1 "Misericordias Domini in aeternum cantabo." Ps. 88.1.
[71] be able to rest satisfied with Your forgiveness only:
give me also a great love for You. Having so often deserved to burn in the fire of hell, I now desire to burn in
the fire of Your holy love. I love You, who are my only
love, my life, my treasure, my all. O Mary, my protectress! pray for me, that I may continue faithful to God
until the end of my life.

MEDITATION 35.
The Soul's Appearance at the Tribunal of God.

1. When criminals are presented before their judges,
though they fear and tremble, yet flatter themselves
that either their crimes will not be proved against them,
or that their judges will remit in part the punishments
which they have deserved. O God! how great will be

the horror of a guilty soul when presented before Jesus Christ, from whom nothing will be hidden, and who will judge it with the utmost severity! *I am the Judge and the Witness*1 will he then say: "I am Your Judge, and I am witness of all the offenses You have committed against me."

My Jesus! I deserved to hear this from Your mouth, had the hour of my judgment arrived. But now You are pleased to assure me, that if I will repent of my sins, You will no longer remember them: *I will not remember all his iniquities.*2

2. It is the opinion of theologians that in the same place in which the soul is separated from the body it will be judged, and its lot decided either for eternal life or eternal death. But should the soul unhappily depart from the body in sin, what will it be able to say when Jesus Christ reminds it of his abused mercies, of the years he granted it, of the calls by which he invited it,

1 "Ego sum judex et testis." Jer. 29.23.
2 Omnium iniquitatum . . . non recordabor." Ezek. 18.22.

[72] and of the many other means which he offered it of securing its salvation?

Jesus, my Redeemer! You who condemn obstinate sinners, do not condemn those who love You and who are sorry for having offended You. I am a sinner, but I love You more than myself, and I am sorry above every evil for having displeased You; oh, do pardon me before the time comes when You will judge me!

3. *At what hour you think not, the Son of man will come.***1**

When, therefore, O my Jesus and my Judge! You shall judge me, after my death, Your wounds will be a terror to me, reproaching me with my ingratitude for the love which You have shown me in suffering and dying for me, but now they encourage me and give me confidence to hope for pardon from You, my Redeemer, who for the love of me, and that You may not have to condemn me, did allow Yourself to be tormented and crucified. *We therefore pray You, help Your servants whom You have redeemed with Your precious blood.***2** O my Jesus! have pity on me, who am one of those sheep for whom You did shed Your sacred blood. If until now I have despised You, I now esteem and love You above all things. Make known to me the means by which I may be saved, and strengthen me to fulfill Your holy will. I will no longer abuse Your goodness. You have placed me under too many obligations to You; I will no longer permit myself to live at a distance from You and be deprived of Your love. Mary, Mother of mercy, have compassion on me.

1 "Qua hora non putatis, Filius hominis veniet." Luke 12.40.

2 Te ergo quaesumus, tuis famulis subveni, quos pretioso sanguine redemisti.

[73] **MEDITATION 36.**
The Unhappy Life of the Sinner.

1. *There is no peace for the wicked.***1** The devil deceives poor sinners by making them believe that if they gratify their sensual desires, revenge themselves, or take what belongs to another, they will gain satisfaction and obtain peace: but no, for the reverse will always be their portion; the soul after sin becomes more than ever disquieted and afflicted. The brutes alone, who are created for the earth, can gain contentment from the enjoyments of the earth; but man, who is created to enjoy God, cannot derive satisfaction from any or all of God's creatures; his only source of happiness is God.

My God! what, of all the delights by which I have offended You, now remains but bitterness and sorrow to torment me? I do not regret the bitterness which they now cause me; but only the displeasure which they have given You, who have so much loved me.

2. *The wicked are like the raging sea, which cannot rest.***2** What is a soul in disgrace with God but a tempestuous sea, always in agitation? one wave rises and another succeeds, and all are waves of pain and anguish. No

one in the world can have all things according to his will. He who loves God, when adversity comes resigns himself to God's blessed will, and thus secures peace to his soul; but how can the sinner, if he is an enemy of God, pacify himself by resignation to God's holy arrangements? Besides, sin always brings with it the dread of divine vengeance. *The wicked man flees, when no man pursues.***3** Yes, for his own sin follows after

1 "Non est pax impiis, dicit Dominus ." Isaiah 48.22.
2 "Impii quasi mare fervens, quod quiescere non potest." Isaiah 57.20.
3 "Fugit impius, nemine persequente." Prov. 28.1.

[74] him, and by the remorse with which it preys upon his soul, makes him suffer an anticipated hell.

O my Lord and my God! I am exceedingly sorry for having forsaken You; do forgive me, and do not permit me to lose You any more.

3. *Delight in the Lord, and He will give you the requests of your heart.***1** Man, where are you going in search of contentment? Seek after God, and he will satisfy all the desires of Your soul. "Seek," says St. Augustine, "the one only good, in whom are all other goods."**2** Behold a St. Francis, who when stripped of all worldly goods, being still united with God, found in this a heaven even here upon earth, and could not often enough exclaim, "My God! my God and my all!" : Happy the soul that leaves all for God, for in him it finds all.

Jesus! instead of abandoning me, as I have deserved, You offer me pardon, and call me to Your Love. Behold, I return to You overwhelmed with sorrow for the evil which I have done, and deeply affected at seeing that even still You love me after the many offenses I have committed against You. You love me, and I also love You and love You more than myself. Receive me into Your favor, and do with me what You please: only do not deprive me of Your love. Mary, Mother, have pity on me.

MEDITATION 37.
The Love of Jesus Crucified.

1. Well might our loving Redeemer declare that he came upon the earth to enkindle divine love, and that he desired nothing else but to see this sacred fire burn-

1 "Delectare in Domino, et dabit tibi petitiones cordis tui." Ps. 36.4.
2 "Ama unum bonum, in quo sunt omnia bona." *Man.*, ch. 34.
3 Deus meus, Deus meus, et omnia.

[75] ing in our hearts: *I have come to cast fire upon the earth : and what will I but that it be kindled*?**1** And, in fact, how many happy souls have been so inflamed with the thoughts of a crucified God as to forsake all things else to give themselves entirely to his holy love! What more could Jesus Christ have done to induce us to love him than to die in torments upon a cross to prove how

much he loved us? With good reason did St. Francis of Paula, when he contemplated with admiration Jesus crucified, exclaim in an ecstasy of love, "O love! love! love!"

2. But alas, how generally do men live forgetful of so loving a God! If the vilest of men - if a slave had done for me what Jesus Christ has done and suffered for me, how should I be able to live without loving him? O God! who is he that hangs upon the cross? the same that created me and that now dies for me. That cross, those thorns, those nails, exclaim, and with a still louder voice those wounds cry out and demand our love.

3. "May I die," said St. Francis of Assisi, "for the love of Your love, O Jesus! who have died for the love of my love." To make an adequate return for the love of God in dying for us would require another God to die for him. It would be but little, it would be nothing, were each of us to give a thousand lives in return for the love of Jesus Christ. But Jesus is satisfied with our giving him our hearts; nevertheless he is not satisfied unless we give them entirely to him. *For this end*, says the Apostle, *did he die, that he might have the entire dominion of our hearts: That He might be Lord both of the dead and of the living.***2**

My beloved Redeemer, how can I ever more forget

1 "Ignem veni mittere in terram; et quid volo, nisi ut accendatur?" Luke 12.49.
2 "In hoc enim Christus mortuus est et resurrexit, ut et mortuorum et vivorum dominetur." Rom. 14.9.

[76] You? how can I love anything else, after having seen You die in torments on an infamous cross to satisfy for my sins? and how can I reflect that my sins have reduced You to this, and not die with grief at the remembrance of the offenses I have committed against You? Jesus, help me; I desire nothing but You; help me and love me. O Mary, my hope! assist me by Your prayers.

MEDITATION 38.
The Will of God to Save All.

1. The Apostle St. Paul teaches us that God wills the salvation of all: *He wills that all men be saved.***1** and St. Peter says: *the Lord deals patiently for your sake, not willing that any should perish, but that all should return to repentance.***2** For this end the Son of God came down from heaven, and was made man, and spent thirty-three years in labors and sufferings, and finally shed his blood and laid down his life for our salvation; and shall we forfeit our salvation?

You, my Savior, did spend Your whole life in securing my salvation, and in what have I spent so many years of my life? What fruit have You until now reaped from me? I have deserved to be cut off and cast into hell. But You *desire not the death of the sinner, but that he be converted and live.***3** Yes, O God! I leave all and turn myself to You. I love You, and because I love You I am sorry for having offended You. Receive me, and permit me not to forsake You any more.

2. How much did the saints do to secure their eternal salvation! How many nobles and kings have forsaken

1 "Omnes homines vult salvos fieri." 1 Tim. 2.4.
2 "Patienter agit, nolens aliquos perire, sed omnes ad poenitentiam reverti." 2 Peter 3.9.
3 "Nolo mortem impii, sed ut convertatur . . . et vivat." Ezek. 33.11.

[77] their kingdoms and estates, and shut themselves up in cloisters! How many young persons have forsaken their country and friends, and have dwelt in caves and deserts! And how many martyrs have laid down their lives under the most cruel tortures! And why? to save their souls. And what have we done?

Woe to me, who, although I know that death is near at hand, yet think not of it! No, my God, I will no longer live at a distance from You. Why do I delay? Is it that death may overtake me in the miserable state in which I now am? No, my God, do assist me to prepare for death.

3. O God, how many graces has my Savior bestowed on me to enable me to save my soul! He has caused me to be born in the bosom of the true Church; he has

many times pardoned me my transgressions; he has favored me with many lights in sermons, in prayers, in meditations, in Communions, and spiritual exercises; and often has he called me to his love. In a word, how many means of salvation has he granted me which he has not granted others!

And yet, O God! when shall I detach myself from the world and give myself entirely to You? Behold me, O Jesus! I will no longer resist. You have obliged me to love You. I desire to be wholly Yours: do receive me, and disdain not the love of a sinner who has until now so much despised You. I love You, my God, my love, and my all; have pity on me, O Mary! You are my hope.

MEDITATION 39.
The Near Approach of Death.

1. Every one knows that he must certainly die; yet many delude themselves by imagining that death is at so immense a distance from them that it will scarcely [78] ever reach them. No; our life is indeed short, and death is very near us. The days of our sojourning here are few, and perhaps much fewer than we imagine. What else is our life but a light vapor, which is driven away and disappears with the wind? a blade of grass which is dried up in the heat of the sun?

O God! You would not allow death to overtake me when I was under Your displeasure, because You did love me and did desire my salvation; and so I will also love You.

2. *My days*, said holy Job, *have been swifter than a runner.*[1] Death is hastening towards us more rapidly than a runner, and we at every step, and every breath and moment, are drawing nearer and nearer to death. At the time of our death how shall we wish for one day or one hour of the many we now squander away to no purpose!

Ah! Lord, if death were now announced to me, what should I find that I have done for You? Alas! come to my assistance; let me not die ungrateful to You as I until now have been. Grant me true sorrow for my sins, the gift of Your love, and holy perseverance.

3. Death hastens towards us; and so we must also hasten to do that which is good, and to put our accounts in order against the day of its arrival. When death comes it precludes all remedies for what has been done badly. How many are now in hell who thought of amending their lives at some future period, but were prevented by death and consigned to eternal torments!

My dear Redeemer, I will no longer resist Your calls. You offer me pardon, and I am desirous of obtaining it; I pray for it, and hope for it, through that death

which You, my Jesus, have suffered that You may
be able to impart it to me. I am sorry, O infinite goodness, for having offended You. You, my Jesus, have
died for me, and I have put off Your friendship for my

1 "Dies me! velociores fuerunt cursore." Job 9.25.

[79] own wretched inclinations. For the future I hope
with Your assistance always to love You. I love You, O
God! I love You. You are now and shall be forever
my only good, my only love. Mary, mother of God,
watch over me and take pity on me.

MEDITATION 40.
God Abandons the Sinner in his Sins.

1. It is a grievous chastisement of God when he cuts
the sinner off in his sins; but still worse is that whereby
he abandons him and allows him to add sin upon sin.
"No punishment is so great," says Bellarmine, "as when
sin is made the punishment of sin."**1**

I give You thanks, therefore, O Jesus! for not having
allowed me to die in my sins; and I give You still
greater thanks for not having abandoned me in my
sins. And oh! into how much deeper an abyss of sin
should I have fallen if you had not supported me.
Continue, O Lord! to keep me from sin and do not

forsake me.

2. *I will take away the hedge thereof, and it shall be wasted.***2** When the master cuts down the fence of his vineyard, and leaves it open for any one to enter there-in, it is a sign that he considers it not worth cultivating, and abandons it. In like manner does God proceed when he forsakes a sinful soul: he takes away from it the hedge of his holy fear, of his light, and of his voice; and from here the soul being blinded and enslaved by its vices, which overpower it, despises everything, the grace of God, heaven, admonitions, and censures; it thinks lightly even of its own damnation, and thus en-

1 "Nulla poena gravior, quam cum peccatum est poena peccati. *In Ps.* 68.
2 "Auferam sepem ejus, et erit in direptionem." Isaiah 5.5.

[80] veloped in darkness is certain to be lost forever. *The wicked man, when he has come into the depths of sins, scorns it.***1**

This have I deserved, O God! for having so often de-spised Your light and Your calls. But I see that You have not yet abandoned me. I love You, O my God! and in You do I place all my hopes.

3. *We would have cured Babylon, but she is not healed; let us forsake her.***2** The physician visits the sick man, pre-scribes remedies for him, and makes him sensible of his

maladies; but when he sees that his patient does not obey him, and on this account grows worse and worse, he takes leave of him and forsakes him. It is thus that God deals with obstinate sinners: after a certain time he speaks but little to them; and only assists them with grace just sufficient to enable them to save their souls; but they will not save them. The darkness of their minds, the hardness of their hearts, and the inveteracy of their wicked habits, render it morally impossible for them to gain salvation.

But, O God! since You still call me to repentance, You have not yet abandoned me; I desire never more to forsake You. I love You, O infinite goodness! and because I love You I am exceedingly sorry for having offended You. I love You, and I hope through Your blood to love You forever. Do not allow me to be any more separated from You. Holy Mary, Virgin of virgins, become my advocate.

MEDITATION 41.
The Examination at the Particular Judgment.

1. In the same moment and in the same place in which the soul departs from the body, the divine tribunal

1 "Impius, cum in profundum venerit peccatorum, contemnit." Prov. 18.3.
2 "Curavimus Babylonem, et non est sanata; derelinquamus." Jer. 51.9.

[81] is erected, the indictment read, and the sentence pronounced by the sovereign judge. *Those whom he foreknew,* says St. Paul, *he also predestined to be made conformable to his Son . . . them he also justified.***1** In order, therefore, to be made worthy of glory, our lives must be made conformable to the life of Jesus Christ. Hence it is that St. Peter says that, in the day of judgment, the just man shall scarcely be saved.**2**

Jesus, my Savior and my judge! what will become of me, since my whole life has until now been the reverse of Yours? But Your Passion is my hope. I am a sinner, but You can make me a saint, and this I hope for from Your generosity.

2. The Venerable Father Louis da Ponte, reflecting on the account which he should have to give of his whole life at the time of his death, trembled to such a degree as to make the whole room shake. And how ought we to tremble at the thought of this account! and how diligent ought we to be in seeking the Lord while we may find him! At the time of death it will be difficult to find him, if we are overtaken in our sins; but now we may easily find him by repentance and love.**3**

Yes, my God, I am sorry above every evil for having despised You; and I now esteem and love You above every good.

3. What shall I do, said holy Job, when God shall rise to judge? and when He shall examine, what shall I answer Him?**4** And what shall I answer him, if, after so many mercies, so many calls, still I resist him?

1 "Quos praescivit et praedestinavit conformes fieri imaginis Filii sui . . . illos et glorificavit." Rom. 8.29.
2 "Justus vix salvabitur." 1 Peter 4.18.
3 "Quaerite Dominum, dum inveniri potest." Isaiah 55.6.
4 "Quid faciam, cum surrexerit ad judicandum Deus? Et cum quaesierit, quid respondebo illi?" Job 31.14.

[82] No, Lord, I will no longer resist You, I will no longer be ungrateful to You. I have committed many offenses and disloyalties against You, but You have shed Your blood to save me from my sins. *"Help Your servant whom You have redeemed with Your precious blood."***1** I am sorry, my sovereign good, for having offended You, and I love You with my whole heart; have pity on me. And O Mary, my Mother, do not abandon me!

MEDITATION 42.
The Journey to Eternity.

1. *Man shall go into the house of his eternity.***2** This earth is not our true country; we are only passing through it on our way to eternity. The land in which I dwell, the house which I inhabit, are not mine. In a short time,

and when I least expect it, I must leave them. The house which will contain my body until the day of general judgment will be the grave, and the house of my soul will be eternity, in heaven if I be saved, in hell if I be lost. Foolish indeed, then, should I be were I to place my affections on things which I must soon leave. I will endeavor to procure for myself a happy mansion in which I may dwell forever.

2. Man shall go into the house of his eternity. It is said "he shall go," to give us to understand that each one shall go, in another life, into that house which he himself has chosen: "he shall go," he shall not be conducted, but shall go there of his own free will. Faith teaches us that in the next life there are two habitations: one is a palace of delights, where all are happy forever, and this is paradise; the other is a prison of excruciating torments, where all are forever miserable, and this is hell. Choose, my soul, to which of the two you will go.

1 Tuis famulis subveni, quos pretioso sanguine redemisti.
2 "Ibit homo in domum aeternitatis suae." Eccles. 12.5.

[83] If You desire heaven, you must walk in the way which leads to heaven; if you should walk in the way which leads to hell, you will one day unhappily find yourself there.

Jesus, enlighten me; Jesus, strengthen me. Permit me

not to be separated from You.

3. Man shall go into the house of his eternity. If then I be saved and enter into the house of bliss, I shall therebe happy forever; but if I be lost and enter into the house of woe, I shall be miserable forever. If, therefore, I would be saved, I must keep eternity always before my eyes. He who frequently meditates upon eternity does not become attached to the goods of this world, and thus secures his salvation. I will endeavor, therefore, so to regulate all my actions that they may be so many steps towards a happy eternity.

O God! I believe in life eternal. Henceforth I will live only for You; until now I have lived for myself and have lost You, my sovereign good. I will never more lose You; but will forever serve and love You. Assist me, O Jesus! and do not abandon me. Mary, my Mother, protect me.

MEDITATION 43.
Jesus, the Man of Sorrows.

1. The prophet Isaiah calls our Blessed Redeemer a man of sorrows;**1** and such he was, for his whole life was a life of sorrows. He took upon his own shoulders all our debts. It is true that as he was man and God, a single prayer from him would have been sufficient to

make satisfaction for the sins of the whole world; but
our Savior would rigorously satisfy divine justice, and
from here he chose for himself a life of contempt and suffering, being content for the love of man to be treated as

1 "Virum dolorum." Isaiah 53.3.

[84] the last and the vilest of men, as the prophet Isaiah
had foreseen him: *We have seen Him . . . despised and the
most abject of men.***1**

O my despised Jesus! by the contempt which You did
endure You have made satisfaction for the contempt
with which I have treated You. Oh that I had died and
had never offended You!

2. Who, my God, among the sons of men, was ever
so afflicted and oppressed as our most loving Redeemer?
Man, however much he may be afflicted in this world,
enjoys from time to time relief and consolation. Thus
does our compassionate God treat his ungrateful and
rebellious creatures. But he would not thus treat his
beloved Son; for the life of Jesus Christ in this world
was not only a life of afflictions, but of continual afflictions from its commencement until death. Our Blessed
Savior was deprived of all consolation and of every
kind of relief. In a word, he was born only to suffer and
to be the man of sorrows.

O Jesus! how unhappy is he who does not love You,

or who loves You but little, after You have so loved
us miserable worms who have offended You! Enable
me from this day forward to love no other but You,
who alone are worthy of being loved.

3. Again, men suffer afflictions, but it is only while
they are suffering them, because they do not know those
which are yet to come. But Jesus Christ, having, as
God, a knowledge of all future things, suffered in every
moment of his life, not only the pains which actually
afflicted him, but all those also which were to come upon
him, and especially the outrages of his most sorrowful
Passion, having always before his eyes his scourging
at the pillar, his crowning with thorns, his crucifixion
and bitter death, with all the sorrows and desolation
which accompanied it.

1 "Vidimus eam . . , despectum et novissimum virorum." Isaiah 53.2.

[85] And why, O Jesus! did You suffer so much for
me who have so grievously offended You? Receive
me now that I may love You, and that henceforward I
may love no other but You. My love and my only
good, receive me and strengthen me. I am resolved
to become holy, that I may please You alone. You
desire me to be all Yours, and such do I desire to be.
Holy Mary, You are my hope.

MEDITATION 44.
The Folly of Neglecting Salvation.

1. *What does it profit a man,* says our Lord, *if he gain the world, and suffer the loss of his own soul?* How many rich men, how many nobles, how many monarchs, are now in hell! What now remains to them of their riches and honors but remorse and rage, which prey upon their souls, and will continue to prey upon them for all eternity?

O my God! enlighten me and assist me. I hope never more to be deprived of Your grace. Have pity on a sinner who desires to love You.

2. How is it, writes Salvian, that men believe in death, judgment, hell, and eternity, and yet live without fearing them? Hell is believed, and yet how many go down there! But, O God! while these truths are believed, they are not dwelt upon, and from this are so many souls lost.

Alas! I also have been of the number of those who have been guilty of such folly. Although I knew that by offending You I was forfeiting Your friendship and writing my own condemnation, yet I was not restrained from committing sin! *"Cast me not away from Your face!"*[1] I am sensible of the evil I have done in despising You, my God, and am grieved for it with my whole soul. Oh, "cast me not away from Your face."

1 Ps 50.13

[86] 3. And then? and then? Oh, what force have these
two words with Fr. P. Francis Zazzera when repeated to
him by St. Philip Neri, in order to induce him to renounce the world and give himself wholly to God!* *Oh
that they would be wise, and would understand, and
would provide for their ultimate end.*1 Oh! if all persons
would but think of death, in which everything must be
relinquished; of judgment, in which an account must be
given of our whole lives; of a happy or miserable eternity,
which must be the lot of each one : if all did but provide
for these last things of their lives, no one would be lost.
The present only is thought of, and from here is eternal
salvation lost.

I give You thanks, O God, for the patience with
which You have until now borne with me, and for
the light which You now bestow upon me. I see
that although I forgot You, You did not forget me.
I am sorry, my sovereign good, for having turned my
back upon You, and I am now resolved to give myself
entirely to You. And why should I delay? That You
may abandon me, and that death may find me as miserable and ungrateful as I have been even until now?

* The circumstance to which St. Alphonsus here refers is thus
related by him in his sermon for Septuagesima Sunday:

"St. Philip Neri, speaking one day to a young man named Francis
Zazzera, who expected to make his fortune in the world by his talents,

said : Be of good heart, my son; you may make a great fortune, you may become an eminent lawyer, you may then be made a bishop, then perhaps a cardinal, and then, who knows, perhaps even Pope. And then? and then? Go, continued the Saint, and reflect upon these two words. The young man went his way, and after having meditated on the two words *and then? and then?* abandoned all his worldly prospects, and gave himself entirely to God. Leaving the world, he entered into the same congregation that St. Philip had founded, and then he died in the odor of sanctity."

1 "Utinam saperent, et intelligerent, ac novissima providerent." Deut. 32.29.

[87] No, my God, I will no more offend You, but will love You. I love You, O infinite goodness! Give me perseverance and Your holy love; I ask for nothing more. Mary, refuge of sinners, intercede for me.

MEDITATION 45.
The Moment of Death.

1. "*O moment, on which depends eternity!*"**1** - Oh! how much depends on the last moment of our lives, on our last breath! Either an eternity of delights, or an eternity of torments , a life of happiness, or a life of misery. What folly therefore must it be, for the sake of a wretched momentary pleasure in this life, to run the risk of making an evil end, and beginning a life of misery which will never terminate!

O God! what will become of me in the last moment of my life? O Jesus, who did die for my salvation! permit me not to be lost forever; permit me not to lose You, my only good.

2. O God! how do those miserable criminals who are condemned to cast lots for their lives tremble when they throw the dice, upon the cast of which depends their life or death! Tell me, Christian, if you were in such a situation, how much you would give to be liberated from it? But faith teaches you that you will one day arrive at that last moment, on which will depend your eternal life or death. You will then say, "Alas! I must now be either happy forever with God, or in despair forever without him."

No, my God, I will not lose You; if I have until now forfeited Your friendship, I am sorry for it, and sincerely repent of it; I will never lose You again.

3. Either we believe, or we do not believe. And if we believe that there is an eternity, that we can die only

1 O momentum, a quo pendet aeternitas!

[88] once, and that if we die badly, the consequences will be eternal, without the least hope of remedy; why do we not resolve to separate ourselves from all danger of being lost, and to use all the means in our power to secure for

ourselves a happy death? No security can be too great when eternity is at stake. The days of our lives are so many favors from God, by which he allows us time to prepare our accounts against the arrival of death. Delay not, for you have no time to lose.

Behold me, O God! tell me what I must do to be saved, for I will do all that You require of me. I have turned my back upon You; and for this I am exceedingly sorry, and for having done so would willingly die of grief. Pardon me, O Lord! and permit me not to forsake You any more. I love You above all things, and will never more cease to love You. Holy Mary, Virgin of virgins, obtain for me the grace of perseverance in virtue.

MEDITATION 46.
The Desire of God to Save Sinners.

1. It is indeed very surprising that man, a worm of the earth, should dare to offend his Creator and turn his back upon him, by despising his graces after God has so favored and loved him as to lay down his life to save him. But it is still more surprising that God, after having been thus despised by man, should seek after him, invite him to repentance and offer him his pardon, as though God stood in need of us and not we of him.

Jesus! You seek me, and I seek after You.

You desire me, and I desire only You.

2. *For Christ*, says the Apostle, *we beseech you, be reconciled to God.***1** "And does God, "exclaims St. John

1 "Obsecramus pro Christo, reconciliamini Deo." 2 Cor. 5.20.

[89] Chrysostom, "call thus upon sinners? And what does he ask of them? to be reconciled, and be in peace with him."**1**

My Redeemer, Jesus Christ, how could You have had so much love for me, who have so often offended You? I detest all my offenses against You; give me still greater grief, still greater love, that I may deplore my sins, not so much on account of the punishments I have deserved by them, as for the injury I have offered to You, my God, who are infinitely good and amiable.

3. *What is man*, exclaims holy Job, *that You should magnify him? or why do You set Your heart upon him?***2**

What good, O Lord! have You ever derived from me? and what can You expect from me, that You love me so much, and come so near to me? Have You then forgotten all the injuries and treasons which I have committed against You? But since You have so much loved me, I, a miserable worm, must also love You, my Creator and my Redeemer. Yes, I do love You, my

God; I love You with my whole heart, I love You more than myself, and because I love You I will do everything to please You. You know that nothing is so grievous to me as the remembrance of my having so often despised Your love. I hope for the future to be able to compensate by my love for the frequent displeasure which I have given You. Help me for the sake of that precious blood which You have shed for me. Help me also, O holy Mary! for the love of Your Son who died for me.

MEDITATION 47.
The Sentence of Particular Judgment.

1. Oh! what joy will he experience who, departing out of this life in the grace of God, will, on being pre-

1 "Ipse Christus vos obsecrat; quid autem obsecrat? reconciliamini Deo." *In 2 Cor.*, hom. 2.
2 "Quid est homo, quia magnificas eum? aut quid apponis erga eum cor tuum? Job 7.17.

[90] sented before Jesus Christ, behold him with a kindly countenance, be lovingly received by him, and hear from him those delightful words: *Well done, good and faithful servant : because you have been faithful over a few things, I will place you over many things: enter into the joy of your Lord.*1

But, O Jesus! if I were now to be summoned to judgment before You, how could I hope that You would call me a good and faithful servant, when I have until now been so bad and faithless towards You, changing my promises of fidelity into betrayals? But I will be faithful to You for the future, and will sooner lose my life a thousand times than forfeit Your grace. Do give me strength to fulfill this my resolution.

2. On the other hand, what anguish, O Jesus! will that sinner experience, who, dying in sin, and being presented before You, beholds Your wrathful countenance! The soul that departs this life in God's displeasure will first condemn itself, and will then hear from Jesus Christ that terrible sentence: *Depart from me, You accursed, into everlasting fire.***2**

How often, O Jesus, have I deserved to hear from You the same sentence when I have committed mortal sin! When death overtakes me, You will then be my judge; but now You are my Father and Redeemer, ready to pardon me, if I am sorry for having offended You. I am therefore sorry, from the bottom of my heart, for all my offenses against You; and I am sorry, not so much on account of hell which I have deserved by them, as because by them I have grievously offended You, who have loved me with an infinite love.

3. The soul goes forth and leaves the body, but it is for
1 "Euge, serve bone et fidelis; quia super pauca fuisti fidelis, super

multa te constituam: intra in gaudium Domini tui." Matt. 25.23.
2 "Discede a me, maledicte, in ignem aeternum." Matt. 25.41.

[91] some time doubtful whether the person be alive or dead. While the bystanders are doubting, the soul has already entered eternity. The priest, satisfied at length that the man is dead, recites the prayer of the Church: "Come to his assistance, all ye saints of God: meet him, all you angels of God: receive his soul and present it now before its Lord."1 But of what avail will it be to the soul that has departed an enemy of God, and upon which sentence has already been passed, to call the saints and angels to its assistance?

My good angel, you saints, my holy advocates, St. Michael, St. Joseph, and you my holy protectress Mary! help me now while you have it in your power. And You, my Redeemer, pardon me now while You exercise mercy. I am sorry for having offended You, and I love You with my whole heart. Assist me, O Lord! and support me, that I may never offend You again. O Mary! take me forever into Your care.

MEDITATION 48.
An Unprovided Death.

1. Nothing is more certain than death, but nothing more uncertain than the hour of death. It is certain that the year and day of each one's death are already determined by

our Lord, though we know them not; and wisely does
God conceal them from us, in order that we may always
prepare for our departure.

I give You thanks, O Jesus! for having waited for
me, and for not having called me out of life in the state
of mortal sin. During the remainder of my life I will
weep for my iniquities and love You with all my strength.
I know that I must die, and by Your grace I will prepare
myself for a good death.

1 Subvenite Sancti Dei. Occurrite, Angeli Domini, suscipiente
animam ejus, offerentes eam in conspectu Altissimi.

[92] 2. Jesus Christ admonishes us of the hour of our
death, and when will it be? when we least expect it.
*At what hour you think not, the Son of man will come.*1
If then, says St. Bernard, death may at any time take us
out of life, we should at all times be prepared for it and
keep our accounts in order.

O Jesus! I will not wait until the moment of my death
to give myself to You. You have said that those who
seek You shall find You: *Seek and you shall find.*2 I
seek You, I desire You; grant that I may find You. I am
sorry for my sins and will nevermore offend You.

3. When then, dear Christian, you are tempted to commit sin with the hope of confessing it the next day,

say to yourself: But who knows but that this moment may be my last? And if in this moment I should be guilty of sin, and death should overtake me, where would I go? O God! how many miserable sinners have been struck by death in the act of feasting themselves on some poisonous gratification! The devil will say to you: This misfortune will not befall you. But do you answer him: If it should befall me, what will become of me for eternity?

God! may it not happen to me which has happened to so many other unhappy sinners? How many are now in hell for lesser sins than I have committed! I give You thanks, O Jesus! for having waited for me with so much patience, and for having now enlightened me. I have erred in forsaking You; and death might have been my punishment; but since You give me time, henceforward I will think of nothing but of loving You. Assist me with Your grace. And do You, Mary, assist me by Your holy intercession.

1 "Qua hora non putatis, Filius hominis veniet." Luke 12.40.
2 "Quaerite, et invenietis." Matt. 7.7.

MEDITATION 49.
The Eternity of Hell.

[93] 1. If hell were not eternal, it would not be hell. Pun-

ishment that does not continue for a long time is not grievous punishment. On the other hand, punishment, however light it may be, when it continues for a long time, becomes intolerable. Were a person obliged during the whole of his life to see the same entertainments, or to hear the same music, how could he endure it? What then must it be to remain in hell and to suffer all its torments! And for how long a time? For all eternity. It would be folly, for the sake of a day's pleasure, to condemn one's self to be burnt alive. And is it not folly, for the sake of a sensual gratification, which can last but for one moment, to condemn one's self to the fire of hell, whose victims, though dying every moment, yet never, never die?

O God! preserve me by Your grace. Woe to me if I should turn my back upon You after the great mercy with which You have dealt with me! Keep me, O God! and preserve me from so great a misfortune.

2. Let us awaken our slumbering faith. It is certain that he who is lost is lost forever, without the least hope of being redeemed from eternal ruin. *They shall go into eternal punishment.***1** He who once enters the prison of hell can come out no more. Otherwise the condemned wretches would flatter themselves with hopes, and would say, Who knows, perhaps God may some day have pity on us and deliver us? But no, they well know that hell will never have an end, and that they must continue to

suffer the same torments that they at present endure so long as God shall be God. My dear Redeemer, I know too well that by the past I have forfeited Your grace, and

1 "Ibunt hi in supplicium aeternum." Matt. 25.46.

[94] condemned myself to hell; but I do not know whether You have pardoned me. Hasten to forgive me, O Jesus! while I bitterly lament my offenses against You, and never permit me to offend You any more.

3. In this life death is of all things the most dreaded, but in hell it is of all things the most desired. There they desire and long for death, but cannot die. *They shall desire to die, and death shall fly from them.*1 Are there not at least, in that place of torments, some to compassionate them? No, all hate them, and rejoice in their sufferings, which will last forever, without end of mitigation. The trumpet of divine justice continually sounds and thunders forth in their ears those terrible words: "Forever, forever; never, never."

Amongst these miserable beings, O Jesus! I have deserved to be numbered; but You, who have until now preserved me from falling into hell, preserve me for the future from falling into sin, which alone can condemn me to that place of woe. Ah! never permit me again to become Your enemy. I love You, O infinite goodness! and I am sorry for having offended You. Pardon me, and as I have deserved to burn forever in the fire of hell, grant me to burn forever with the fire of Your holy love. O Mary, in Your powerful intercession do I confide.

MEDITATION 50.
The Uncertainty of Grace.

1 . *Delay not to be converted to the Lord, and put it not off from day to day: for His wrath shall come suddenly, and in the time of vengeance will He destroy You.***2** The Lord admonishes us to be speedily converted, if we would be

1 "Desiderabunt mori, et fugiet mors ab eis." Rev. 9.6.
2 "Non tardes converti ad Dominum, et ne differas de die in diem: subito enim veniet ira illius, et in tempore vindictae disperdet te." Eccles. 5.9.

[95] saved; because if we go on putting off our conversion from day to day, the time of vengeance will come, when God will neither call nor wait for us any longer; death will overtake us in sin, and there will be no means of escaping eternal damnation. God admonishes us in this manner, because he loves us and wills not to see us perish. I am convinced, O God! that You desire my salvation; I know that You desire to deal with me in Your mercy; and it is my desire never more to despise You.

2. Alas! to how many have the admonitions given by God during life become now in hell the most cruel

swords that pierce their souls! In proportion as the mercies which God showed them were greater, so were their crimes more enormous.

If, O Jesus! You have condemned me to hell, as I have deserved, how great would have been my punishment, since Your graces and favors have been so abundant towards me! No, I will no longer be ungrateful to You. Say to me what You please, and I will obey You in all things. I am sorry for having so often offended You; henceforward I will not seek to please myself, but to please only You, my God and only good.

3. How cautious are men in their temporal affairs, and yet how negligent in the affairs of eternity! If a man has to receive a sum of money from another, he uses every expedient to obtain it as quickly as possible, say ing, "Who knows what may happen?" And yet, why do so many live months and years in sin? Because they do not say, when the soul is at stake, "Who knows what may happen?" If money be lost, however valuable it may be, all is not lost; but if the soul be lost, all is lost, and must be lost forever, without hope of recovery.

My beloved Redeemer, You have given me life that I may become worthy of Your grace; and yet I have often renounced Your grace for something worse than nothing. Pardon me, O infinite goodness! for I am sorry, from [96] the bottom of my heart, for having done so. O Jesus!

You have done too much to oblige me to love You, and I desire to love You to the utmost of my power. I love You, my sovereign good, I love You more than myself. Permit me not, O God! to cease to love You any more. O Mary, holy queen! protect me.

MEDITATION 51.
The Death of Jesus for the Love of Men.

1. Was it ever possible that God, the Creator of all things, should have been pleased to die for the love of his creatures? Our faith tells us that he has done so. *He has loved us, and has delivered Himself for us.***1** The earth, the heavens, and all nature, with astonishment beheld Jesus, the only begotten Son of God, the lord of the universe, die of intense pain and anguish, on a shameful cross; and why? For the love of men. And do men believe this and not love God?

I have believed it, O Jesus! and yet not only have I not loved You, but I have frequently offended You. Pardon me, I beseech You, and remind me continually of the death which You have suffered for me, that I may never more offend You, but may always love You.

2. It was not necessary for man's salvation that God should die; one drop of his blood, a single tear, or a prayer would have been sufficient, because being of in-

finite value, it would have redeemed this or a thousand other worlds.

But, O Jesus! You would suffer so much, to teach us Your great love for us. Hence, St. Bonaventure exclaims, but with much greater reason may I exclaim, who have so often offended my Redeemer: "Alas! my God, why have You so much loved me? why, O Lord, why? Who am I?" O divine Pastor of my soul, behold

1 "Dilexit nos, et tradidit semetipsum pro nobis." Eph. 5.2.

[97] I am the lost sheep, in quest of which You came upon the earth. I have ungratefully fled away from You; since, unmindful of the sufferings which I have occasioned You, You call me, miserable as I am, but overcome with Your great goodness, embracing Your sacred feet, nailed to the cross. Jesus, my love, my treasure! I love You, and because I love You I am sorry for having offended You.

3. St. Bernard, imagining himself present when Pilate passed sentence of death on our Blessed Savior, thus addresses him: "What have You done, my most innocent Savior, that You should be thus condemned?1 You are innocence itself; and how do I now behold You condemned to death, even to the death of the cross? What crime have You committed?" And he proceeds to answer, "Your crime is love." As if he had said, Ah! it is Your too great love for us, and not

Pilate, that condemns You to death.

When, my dear Redeemer, I remember the offenses
I have committed against You, it is not hell, which I
have deserved for them, that makes me grieve, but the
love which You have shown me. Ah! my crucified
God, I desire to be henceforth and forever Yours, and
I will love no other but You. Strengthen my weakness,
and make me faithful to You. Holy Mary, mother of
God, enable me to love Jesus; this is the only favor
I ask.

MEDITATION 52.
The Certainty of being either Saved or Lost.

1. *With fear and trembling,* says the Apostle, *work out
your salvation.***2** In order to be saved we should tremble

1 Quid fecisti, innocentissime Salvator, quod sic condemnareris?
2 "Cum metu et tremore vestram salutem operamini." Phil. 2.12.

[98] lest we be lost, for there is no middle way; we must
be either saved or lost forever. He who trembles not is
in great danger of being lost, because he takes but little
care to employ the means of obtaining salvation. God
desires that all should be saved, and he gives to all his
grace; but he requires that all should cooperate for
this end. All desire to be saved; many, because they

will not employ the means of salvation, are lost. St. Philip Neri used to say, *"Heaven is not made for the slothful."*

Enlighten me, O Lord, that I may know what I ought to do, and what to avoid, for I desire to do all that You require of me. I am determined, by Your grace, to save my soul.

2. St. Teresa said to her religious, *"One soul! my daughters, one eternity!"* She meant that in this world we ought not to attend to anything but to the salvation of our souls; because if the soul be lost, all will be lost; and if once lost, will be lost forever. Benedict XII, being asked by a prince for a favor that he could not grant without committing sin, answered the ambassador: *"Tell your prince that if I had two souls I would give him one; but as I have only one, I cannot consent to lose it for his sake."* Thus should we answer the devil or the world when they offer us forbidden fruit.

O God! how often have I lost my soul by forfeiting Your grace! But since You offer me Your pardon, I detest all the offenses I have committed against You, and love You above all things.

3. If only we were fully impressed with the meaning of that great maxim of St. Francis Xavier, *"There is but one evil, and there is but one good in the world!"*

The only evil is damnation; the only good, salvation. No: poverty, infirmity, ignominies are not evils; these when embraced with resignation will increase our glory in heaven. On the other hand, health, riches, and honors [99] are not goods for too many Christians, because they become to them greater occasion of losing their souls.

Save me then, O God! and do with me what You please. You know and will what is best for me. I abandon myself to Your mercy: *Into Your hands, O Lord, I commend my spirit.***1** I am so sorry for having been until now opposed to Your will, as even to die to atone for my offenses; but now I love You, and will nothing but what You will. Grant me Your love, that I may be faithful to You. And Mary, give me Your powerful assistance.

MEDITATION 53.
The Certainty of Death.

1. How is it possible, O God! that there should be any Christians who believe that they must one day die, and that after death an eternity of happiness or misery awaits them; who know that on the moment of death will depend their being happy or miserable forever; and yet adopt not all the means of securing for themselves the blessing of a good death?

Give, O Lord, tears to my eyes that I may bewail my offenses against You! I knew that by offending You I would forfeit Your grace and condemn myself to eternal torments; I knew this, and yet I was not restrained from committing sin. I am sorry, O God! for having dishonored You, by renouncing You for the sake of my own wretched inclinations; have pity on me.

2. If we hear of one dying suddenly who did not live prepared for death, we pity him, and say, "Alas! what has become of his poor soul?" And yet why are we not ourselves prepared at all times to die? It may be that the misfortune of a sudden death may

1 "In manus tuas, Domine, commendo spiritum meum." Ps. 30.6.

[100] happen to us; but whether sooner or later, whether prepared or unprepared, whether we think of it or not, we must one day surrender our souls into the hands of God. The place of execution is already prepared for us, and the malady which is to be our executioner and take us out of the world is stealing upon us; why then do we not endeavor to become daily more and more united with Jesus Christ, who will soon become our Judge?

My dear Redeemer, I hope through the merits of Your death to live and die in Your grace and favor. I love You, O infinite goodness, and I hope to love You always in this life and for all eternity in the next.

3. In every succeeding age, cities and kingdoms are peopled with new beings, and their predecessors buried in their graves. Those who lived here a century ago, where are they now! gone into eternity! And thus, dear reader, in a hundred years from now, even in a much shorter time, neither you nor I will be alive in this world, but we shall be either happy or miserable forever in the next; either saved or lost for all eternity, one or the other will most certainly be our lot.

I may then, O God, either be saved, as I hope I shall be, or I may be lost on account of my sins. And is it possible that I may be lost, and yet not think of adopting every means of securing my salvation? Enlighten me, O Lord! and make known to me what I must do to be saved, for with Your help I will do all that You require of me. I have many times lost my respect for You, my Father, but You have not ceased to love me. I detest all my offenses against You, and I love You, O God! with my whole soul. Give me Your blessing, Father, and never permit me to be again separated from You. Mary, my mother, have pity on me.

MEDITATION 54.
The Vanity of the World.

[101] 1. *Only the grave*, says holy Job, *remains for me.*1 Days and years pass away, pleasures, honors, and riches

pass away, and what will be the end? Death will come and strip us of all, and we shall be buried in the grave to corrupt and moulder into dust, deserted and forgotten by all. Alas! how, in the end of our lives, will the remembrance of all we have acquired in this world serve for nothing but to increase our anguish and our uncertainty of salvation!

Death, O death, never depart from before my eyes. O God, do enlighten me.

2. *My life is cut off as by a weaver.* **2** How many, in the midst of executing their long-contemplated designs, are overtaken by death and deprived of all things! Ah, with what pain and remorse will the goods of this world be regarded, on the bed of death, by those who have been unduly attached to them! To worldlings who are spiritually blind the goods of this present life appear great; but death will discover what they really are: dust, smoke, and vanity. Before the light of this last lamp all the dazzling grandeur of this world will vanish and disappear. he greatest fortunes, the highest honors, when considered on the bed of death, will lose all their value and splendor. The shade of death will obscure even crowns and scepters.

Grant me, O God! Your holy grace, for this alone is all I desire. I am grieved for having ever despised such a treasure. Jesus, have pity on me.

3. Of what avail then will riches be at the hour of death, when nothing will remain for us but a wooden

1 "Solum mihi superest sepulcrum." Job, 17.1.
2 "Praecisa est velut a texente vita mea." Isaiah 38.12.

[102] coffin and a winding-sheet? Of what avail will be the honors which we have acquired, when no others will remain for us but a funeral procession and a tomb, which will not be able to grant us the least satisfaction, if our souls should be lost? And of what avail will the beauty of the body be, when the body itself will become a mass of worms, infect the air with its stench, and excite horror in all who behold it?

My dear Redeemer, although I knew that by sinning I would forfeit Your friendship, yet still I sinned; but I hope for pardon from You who have died to purchase pardon for me. Oh that I had never offended You, my good God! I behold the love which You have shown me; and this increases my grief for having displeased You who are so good a Father. I love You, O Lord! and will never live without loving You; give me perseverance. Mary, my mother, pray to Jesus for me.

MEDITATION 55.
The Provoking of God by Sin.

1. Thus does the royal prophet speak of sinners: *They*

*tempted and provoked the most high God.***1** God is incapable of grief; but were it possible for him to grieve, every sin that men commit would deeply afflict him and deprive him of happiness.

Sin, O God, is the return I have made You for Your love! How often have I renounced Your friendship for the sake of some wretched self-gratification O infinite goodness! because You are such, pardon me my offenses.

2. St. Bernard, moreover, adds that the malice of sin is so great that it would annihilate God, were this possible.**2** If God could die, mortal sin would deprive him

1 "Exacerbaverunt Deum excelsum." Ps. 77.56.
2 "Perimit Deum." *S. 3 in temp. pasc.*

[103] of life. And how? Father Medina answers, "Because it would give him infinite sorrow." How afflicting is it to be injured by those whom we have especially befriended and loved! What then must it be for God to behold man, whom he has favored with so many and so great benefits and loved with so great love, even to shedding his blood and laying down his life, what must it be to behold man turn his back upon him and despise his grace for a mere nothing, for a fit of passion, or a momentary pleasure! Were he capable of grief and sadness, he would die of the bitterness which such conduct

would occasion him.**1**

Dearest Jesus, I am the lost sheep; You are the good shepherd who have laid down Your life for Your sheep; have pity on me, pardon me for all the displeasure which my sins have occasioned You. I am grieved, O Jesus! for having offended You, and love You with my whole soul.

3. It was because our loving Redeemer had our sins constantly before his eyes that his life was so painful and full of bitterness. This was the cause of his sweating blood and suffering the agonies of death in the garden of Gethsemane, where he declared that "his soul was sorrowful even unto death."**2** What made him sweat blood and cast him into so dreadful an agony but the sight of the sins of men?

Give me then, O Jesus, a share of the sorrow which then oppressed You for my sins; grant that it may afflict me during my whole life, and, if You please, even unto death. O Jesus! I desire nevermore to displease You, I will nevermore afflict You, but will love You with all my strength, who are my love, my life, and my only good. Do not allow me to offend You any more. Mary, my hope, have compassion on me.

1 "Destrueret Deum, eo quod esset causa tristitiae infinitae." *De Satisf.* q. 1.
2 "Tristis est anima mea usque ad mortem." Matt. 26.38.

MEDITATION 56.
The Last Judgment.

[104] 1. The last day is called in Scripture *a day of wrath and misery*;**1** and such it will be for all those unhappy beings who have died in mortal sin; for on that day their most secret crimes will be made manifest to the whole world, and themselves separated from the company of the saints, and condemned to the eternal prison of hell, where they will suffer all the agonies of ever dying yet always remaining alive. St. Jerome, in the cave of Bethlehem, devoted to continual prayer and penance, trembled at the bare thought of the general judgment. The Ven. Fr. Juvenal Ancina hearing that sequence for the dead sung, *"Dies irae, dies illa,"* was so struck with the anticipation of judgment that he left the world and embraced a religious life.

O Jesus! what will become of me on that day? Shall I be placed on Your right with the elect, or on Your left with the reprobate? I know that I have deserved to be placed on Your left, but I know also that You will still pardon me, if I repent of my sins: and so I do repent of them with my whole heart, and am resolved rather to die than offend You any more.

2. As this will be a day of calamity and terror for the reprobate, so will it be a day of joy and triumph for the elect; for then, in the sight of all mankind, will the blessed

souls of the elect be proclaimed queens of paradise, and spouses of the immaculate Lamb.

O Jesus! Your precious blood is my hope. Remember not the offenses that I have committed against You, and inflame my whole soul with Your love. I love You, my sovereign good, and I trust that in that day I shall be

1 "Dies irae ... dies calamitatis et miseriae." Zeph. 1. 15.

[105] associated with those loving souls who will praise and love You for all eternity.

3. Choose, my soul; choose now either an eternal crown in that blessed kingdom, where God will be seen and loved face to face in the company of the saints, of the angels, and of Mary the Mother of Jesus; or the prison of hell, where you must weep and lament forever, abandoned by God and by all.

"O Lamb of God who takes away the sins of the world, have mercy on us." O divine Lamb, who, to deliver us from the pains of hell, were pleased to sacrifice Your divine life by a bitter death upon the cross, have compassion on us; but more particularly on me who have more than others offended You. I am sorry above every evil for having dishonored You by my sins, but I hope on that day to honor You before men and angels, by proclaiming Your mercies towards me. O Jesus! help

me to love You; I desire You alone. O Mary, holy
queen! protect me in that day.

MEDITATION 57.
The Intensity of the Pains of Hell.

1. In this life when a person suffers, however great his
sufferings may be, he may, at least occasionally, obtain
some mitigation or repose. A sick man may suffer all
the day long the pains of the most cruel disorders; but,
when night comes, he may perhaps sleep a little and be
somewhat relieved. Not so with the miserable reprobate.
For him there is no relief, no repose. He must weep and
lament forever, he must suffer forever, and suffer
torments the most excruciating, without once having
throughout all eternity one moment of ease or mitigation.

1 Agnus Dei, qui tollis peccata mundi, miserere nobis.

[106] Such, O Jesus! would have been my lot, had You
called me out of life in my sins. Dearest Redeemer, I
refuse not to suffer, but will truly love You.

2. In this life by constantly suffering pain we become
accustomed to it and better able to bear it; time mitigates
sufferings which at first were most grievous to us. But
will the souls in hell, by eternally suffering the torments
which they endure, by the habit of enduring them for

so many years, will they ever find their intensity diminished? No, for the torments of hell are of such a nature that, at the end of a hundred or a thousand years, those souls will experience the same degree of pain from them as when they first descended into that bottomless abyss.

*In You, O Lord, have I hoped, let me never be confounded.***1** I know, O Lord! that I have frequently deserved hell, yet I know likewise that You do not desire the death of the sinner, but that he be converted and live. O my God! I will not continue obstinate, but will repent with my whole soul of all my sins, and will love You more than myself; restore me to life, to the life of Your holy grace.

3. In this life, when a person suffers he has the pity and sympathy of his relatives and friends; and these give at least some comfort. But how miserable would it be for a man in the most excruciating pains to be

upbraided and reproached by his relatives and friends with the misdeeds for which he was suffering, saying to him without pity, "Rave on in rage and despair; you have deserved all you suffer!" The miserable wretches in hell suffer all kinds of torments, suffer them continually without any relief or comfort, and have none to sympathize with them. Not even God can sympathize with them, for they are his enemies; nor Mary, the Mother of

Mercy; nor the angels, nor the saints; on the contrary,

1 "In te, Domine, speravi; non confundar in aeternum." Ps. 30.2.

[107] they rejoice in their sufferings. And, at the same time, what is the conduct of the devils towards the reprobate? They trample upon them and reproach them with the crimes which they have committed against God, and for which they are now most justly punished.

Holy Mary, Mother of God, have pity on me, for You have it now in Your power to take pity on me and to recommend me to Your divine Son. O Jesus! You who did not spare Yourself to have compassion on me, but did die upon the cross for my sake, save me, and may my salvation be to love You forever. I am sorry, O Lord! for having offended You, and will love You with my whole heart.

MEDITATION 58.
The Love of Christ Crucified.

1. Who could have conceived that the Son of God, the Lord of the universe, to show his love for us, would suffer and die upon the cross, if he have not really done so? With reason therefore did Moses and Elijah on Mount Tabor speak of the death of Jesus Christ as of an excess of love.1 And what could be greater excess of love than

for the Creator to die for his creatures?

To make You an adequate return for Your love, my
dear Redeemer, it would be necessary for another God
to die for You. It would therefore be but little, it would
be nothing, were we poor miserable worms of the earth
to give up our whole lives for You, who have given Yours
for us.

2. What should still more excite us to love him is the
ardent desire with which, through the course of his life,
he longed for the hour of his death. By this desire he
indeed proved how great his love was for us. *I have a*

1 "Dicebant excessum ejus, quem completurus erat in Jerusalem."
Luke 9.31.

[108] *baptism,* said he, *with which I am to be baptized; and
how am I constrained until it be accomplished.*1 I must be
baptized with the baptism of my own blood, to wash away
the sins of men, and how am I dying with the desire of my
bitter Passion and death! My soul, lift up your eyes, and behold Your Lord hanging upon a disgraceful cross; behold
the blood which trickles down from his wounds; behold
his mangled body, all inviting you to love him. Your Redeemer in his sufferings would have you love him at least
through compassion.

O Jesus! You did not refuse me Your life and precious

blood, and shall I refuse You anything that You require of me? No, You have given Yourself to me without reserve. I will give myself to You in like manner.

3. St. Francis de Sales, speaking of these words of the Apostle, *The love of Christ impels us* 2 says: "Knowing that Jesus Christ, being true God, has loved us even to the laying-down of his life for us, and this upon a cross, do we not feel our hearts as it were in a press, forcibly straitened, and love expressed from them by a violence which is the more powerful as it is the more amiable?" And he adds: "Why, therefore, do we not cast ourselves upon Jesus Christ crucified, to die on the cross for the love of him who has willingly died upon the cross for the love of us? I will adhere to him, should we say, and will never abandon him; I will die with him, and be consumed in the fire of his love. My Jesus has given himself entirely to me, and I will give myself entirely to him. I will live and die upon his bosom; neither life nor death shall ever separate me from him. O eternal love! my soul seeks You nd espouses You forever."3

1 "Baptismo habeo baptizari, et quomodo coarctor usquedum perficietur?" Luke 12. 50.
2 "Charitas Christi urget nos." 2 Cor. 5. 14.
3 *Love of God*, Bk. 7, ch. 8.

[109] Mary, Mother of God, obtain that I may belong entirely to Jesus Christ.

MEDITATION 59.
The Irretrievable Loss of the Soul.

1. There is no error so fatal in its consequences as the loss of eternal salvation. Other errors may be repaired; if a person lose a situation, he may perhaps in time regain it; if he lose his goods, he may replace them, but if he lose his soul, he has no remedy nor hope of redemption. He can die but once; and if that once his soul be lost, it must be lost forever, and no power can save it for all eternity.

Behold, O God! a wretched sinner prostrate at Your feet, one who for so many years past has deserved to dwell in hell without further hope of salvation, but who now loves You, and is sorry above every other evil for having offended You, and hopes for mercy.
2. Does then nothing remain for the many wretched souls in hell but to lament bitterly, and say, "Therefore we have erred,"**1** and there is no remedy for our error, nor will there be so long as God shall be God?

Ah! my Redeemer, were I in hell, I could nevermore repent, nor love You. I thank You for having borne with me with so great patience, even though I have deserved hell; and now that I am still able to repent and to love You, I do sincerely repent for having offended Your infinite goodness, and love You above all things, more than I love myself. Never permit me, O Jesus! to cease to love You.

3. Oh, what a torment must it be to the souls in hell
to think that they knew their error before they were
lost, and that they are lost entirely through their own
fault! If a person lose a gold ring through carelessness,

1 "Ergo erravimus." Wis. 5. 6.

[110] or a valuable coin, he has no peace for thinking that
he has lost it through his own fault. O God! how great is
the internal torment of the wicked when they exclaim,
"I have lost my soul, I have lost heaven, I have lost my
God; I have lost my all; and this through my own
fault!"

O my dear Savior! I desire never to lose You: if I have
until now lost You, I have done ill; I am sorry for it with
my whole soul, and love You above all things. O Jesus!
You have saved me from hell that I may love You. I
will therefore truly love You. Enable me to compensate
by my love for the offenses which I have committed
against You. Holy Virgin Mary, You are my hope.

MEDITATION 60.
We Must Die.

1. How much is contained in these words, "we must

die!" Christian brother, you must one day certainly die. As your name was one day entered in the baptismal register, so will it one day be entered in the book of the dead, and this day is already determined by Almighty God. As you now speak of the dear memory of your father, or of your uncle, or brother, so will posterity speak of you. As you now frequently hear of the deaths of your friends or acquaintances, so will others hear of your death, and you will be gone into eternity.

O God! what will then become of me? When my body is carried to the church, and Mass said over me, where will be my soul? Enable me, O Lord, to do something for Your service before death overtakes me! How wretched I would be if at this moment it should surprise me!

2. What would you say of a criminal on the way to execution who was looking about him here and there, and attending only to the amusements which happened to be [111] going on? Would you not think him mad, or a man who did not believe his impending fate? Are you not every moment advancing towards death? And what do you think of? You know that you must die, and that you can die only once. You believe that after this life another awaits you which will never end; and that this eternal life will be happy or miserable according as your accounts are found at the day of your judgment; and how can you believe

these truths and attend to anything else than making preparation for a good death?

Enlighten me, O my God, and let the thoughts of death, and of the eternity in which I must dwell, be ever present to my mind.

3. Look at the skeletons heaped up in cemeteries: they are silently saying to you, "What has happened to us will soon overtake you." The same is repeated to you by the portraits of your relatives who are dead, by the letters of their handwriting, by the rooms, the beds, the clothes which they once possessed and used, but which they have now abandoned and left behind for you. All these things remind you of death which is waiting for you.

My crucified Jesus, I will not delay to embrace You till the moment of my death, when Your crucified image will be presented to me; but I will embrace You now and press You to my heart. Until now I have frequently expelled You from my soul, but now I love You more than myself, and am sorry for having despised You. For the future I will be always Yours, and You shall be always mine. This is my hope through Your bitter Passion and death. And this also do I hope for through Your protection, O ever blessed Mary!

MEDITATION 61.
The Love with which God receives the Repentant Sinner.

[112] 1. The kings of the earth reject from their presence
their rebellious subjects when they come to seek for
pardon; but Jesus Christ assures us that he will never
reject any rebellious sinner that penitently casts himself
at his feet: *He who comes to Me I will not cast out.***1**
He despises not the heart that is humble and sorry for
having offended him: *A contrite and humble heart, O
God, You will not despise.***2**

I do not, O Jesus! deserve Your pardon for the offenses
which I have committed against You, but You know that
nothing afflicts me so much as the remembrance of my
having offended You.

2. But how can I be afraid that You, my God, will
cast me off, when You invite me to return to You,
and offer me Your pardon? Return to Me and I will
receive You.**3** How can I doubt, when You promise to
embrace us, when we are converted to You? *Turn
to Me, and I will turn to you.***4** Do not, then, O Lord!
turn Your back upon me, for I will renounce all things,
and turn myself to You, my sovereign good. I have
offended You too long, and will now at least love You.

3. Our good God moreover adds that if the sinner repent
of the evil which he has done, he is willing to forget all his

sins: *If the wicked do penance . . . living he shall live, and shall not die. I will not remember all his iniquities that he has done.***5**

1 "Eum qui venit ad me, non ejiciam foras." John 6.37.
2 "Cor contritum et humiliatum, Deus, non despicies." Ps. 1.19.
3 "Revertere ad me . . . et ego suscipiam te." Jer. 3.1.
4 "Convertimini ad me . . . et convertar ad vos." Zach. 1.3.
5 "Si autem impius egerit poenitentiam . . . vita vivet et non morietur; omnium iniquitatum ejus, quas operatus est, non recordabor." Ezek. 18.21.

[113] My dear Redeemer! I will never forget my sins, that I may always bewail the evil which I have done against You; but I trust and hope that You, as You have promised, will soon forget them, and that my past iniquities will not hinder You from loving me. Have You not said that You love those who love You?**1** Until now I have not loved You, and have deserved Your hatred; but now I will love You and hope that You will no longer reject me; and as You forget what is past, forgive me, unite me to Yourself, and never allow me to be again separated from You. Mary, assist me by Your holy intercession.

MEDITATION 62.
Temptations to Relapse.

1. O Christian! when the devil again tempts you to

sin, telling you that "God is merciful," remember that the Lord "shows mercy towards them that fear him,"**2** and not to them that despise him. "God is merciful," it is true; yet how many does he daily condemn to the torments of hell! "God is merciful," but he is also just. He is merciful to those who repent of their sins, but not to those who abuse his mercy to offend him the more freely. O God, how often have I done this! how often have I offended You because You were good and merciful!

2. The devil will say to you, "As he has pardoned you many past sins, so will he pardon you the sin which you are now about to commit." *No,* you must reply; because he has so often forgiven me, I ought to be the more afraid, that, if I should again offend him, he will no more pardon me, but punish me for all the crimes I have ever committed against him. Attend to the ad-

1 "Ego diligentes me diligo." Prov. 8.17.
2 Et misericordia ejus timentibus eum.

[114] monition of the Holy Spirit: *Say not, I have sinned and what harm has befallen me? for the most High is a patient rewarder.***1**

O God! how basely have I corresponded with Your favors! You have bestowed graces upon me, and I have requited them with injuries; You have loaded me with blessings, and I have insulted and dishonored

You. But for the future it shall not be so. The more
You have borne with me, so much the more will I love
You. Do assist my weakness.

3. The devil will say to you: "But do you not see
that you cannot now resist this temptation?" Answer
him: But if I do not resist now, how shall I be able to
resist afterwards, when I shall have become weaker,
and the divine assistance will fail me? Am I to be told
that in proportion as I multiply the number of my sins,
God will multiply the number of his graces towards
me? Finally, he will say to you: "But although you
were to commit this sin, you may still be saved." Say
to him in reply: I may be saved; but is this a reason
why I should write my own sentence of condemnation
to hell? I may be saved; but I may also be lost, and this
is more probable. This is not an affair to be left to the
chance of a "maybe."

But, O Lord! how much have You done for me? I
have multiplied my faults, and You have increased Your
graces! The thought of this embitters my sorrow for
having so heinously offended You. My good God, why
have I offended You? Oh that I could die of grief!
Help me, O Jesus! for I desire to be wholly Yours.
Holy Mary, obtain for me perseverance in virtue, and
permit me not any more to live ungrateful to God who
has so much loved me.

MEDITATION 63.
The Resurrection of the Body.

[115] 1. A day will come which will be the last of days, when this world will be no more. Before the coming of the Judge, fire will descend from heaven, and consume everything that is upon the earth : *The earth and the works which are in it shall be burnt up.***1** So that in that day everything upon the earth will be reduced to ashes. O God! what will all the vanities of this world then appear, for which so many now sacrifice the salvation of their souls? What appearance will all the highest dig-nities of this earth then make, its purple, its crowns, and its scepters? O the folly of those who shall have loved them! And O the lamentations of those who for the love of such vanities shall have lost their God!

2. *The trumpet shall sound, and the dead shall rise again.***2** This trumpet will call all men together from their graves to come to judgment. Oh how beautiful and re-splendent will the bodies of the just appear! *Then shall the just shine like the sun.***3** On the contrary, how ugly and deformed will the bodies of the reprobate appear! What a torment will it be to these wretched souls to be again united with their bodies, for whose gratification

they have lost heaven and lost their God, to be cast with them forever into hell, there to burn together in eternal flames! Happy will they then be who have denied their bodies all gratifications displeasing to God; and who, in order to hold them in greater subjection, have mortified them by fasting and penance!

Jesus! *turn not Your face away from me*, as I have deserved.4 How often, for the sake of gratifying my

1 "Terra et quae in ipsa sunt opera exurentur." 2 Peter 3.10.
2 "Canet tuba, et mortui resurgent." 1 Cor. 15.52
3 "Tunc justi fulgebunt sicut sol." Matt. 13.43.
4 "Non avertas faciem tuam a me." Ps. 142.7.

[116] senses, have I renounced Your friendship! Oh that I had died rather than have thus dishonored You! Have pity on me.

3. All mankind being assembled together, will be summoned by angels to appear in the valley of Josaphat, there to be publicly judged before all: Nations, nations in the valley of destruction? O my God! and must I appear in that valley? In what place shall I stand there? with the elect in glory, or with the reprobate in chains? My beloved Redeemer, Your precious blood is my only hope. Woe to me! how often have I deserved to be condemned to dwell forever in hell, far, far from You, without being able to love You! No, rny Jesus! I will love You forever, in this life and in the next.

Permit me not to be ever again separated from You by sin. You know my weakness; be You always my help, O Jesus! and do not abandon me. Mary, my advocate, obtain for me the gift of holy perseverance.

MEDITATION 64.
The Love of God in Giving us His Son.

1. So great was God's love for us that, after having loaded us with gifts and graces, he bestowed upon us his own Son: *God so loved the world as to give His only begotten Son.*2 For us poor miserable worms of the earth, the eternal Father sent his beloved Son into this world to lead a poor and despised life, and to undergo the most ignominious and bitter death that any mortal on earth had ever suffered, an accumulation of internal as well as eternal torments, such as to cause him to exclaim when dying, "My God, my God, why have You

1 "Populi populi in valle concisionis "Joel 3.14.
2 "Sic Deus dilexit mundum, ut Filium suum unigenitum daret."
John 3.16.

[117] forsaken Me?"1 O eternal God! who but Yourself, who are a God of infinite love, could have bestowed upon us a gift of such infinite value? I love You, O infinite goodness! I love You, O infinite love!

2. *He spared not even His own Son, but delivered Him*

up for us all. 2 But, O God eternal! consider that this
divine Son, whom You doom to die, is innocent,
and has ever been obedient to You in all things. You
love him even as Yourself, how then can You condemn him to death for the expiation of our sins? The
eternal Father replies : "It was precisely because he
was my Son, because he was innocent, because he was
obedient to me in all things, that it was my will he
should lay down his life, in order that you might know
the greatness of that love which we both bear towards
you."

May all creatures forever praise You, O God! for
the excess of bounty through which You have caused
Your own Son to die for the deliverance of us Your
servants. For the love of this Your Son, have pity on
me, pardon me, and save me; and let my salvation be
to love You forever, both in this world and in the next.

3. *But God (who is rich in mercy) for His too great love
with which He loved us . . . has brought us to life together in Christ.***3** Too great, says the Apostle, too great
has been the love of God towards us. We by sin were
dead, and he raised us to life again by the death of his
Son. But no, such love was not too great for the infinite
bounty of our God. Being infinite in all perfection, he
was infinite in love.

1 "Deus meus, Deus meus, ut quid dereliquisti me?" Matt. 27.46.

2 "Proprio Filio suo non pepercit, sed pro nobis omnibus tradidit illum." Rom. 8.32.
3 "Deus autem, qui dives est in misericordia propter nimiam charitatem suam qua dilexit nos, et cum essemus mortui peccatis, convivificavit nos in Christo." Eph. 2.4.

[118] But, O Lord! how is it that after You have shown such love towards men, there are so few who love You? How much do I desire to become one of the number of these few! Until now I have not known You, my sovereign good, but have forsaken You; I am sorry for it from the bottom of my heart, and will so love You that, though all should leave You, I will never forsake You, my God, my love, and my all. O Mary! unite me ever more and more to my dearest Savior.

MEDITATION 65.
Earnest Labor to Secure Eternal Salvation.

1. To be saved it is not sufficient to profess merely to do what is absolutely necessary. If, for example, a person wishes to avoid only mortal sins, without making any account of those which are venial, he will easily fall into mortal sins and lose his soul. He who desires to avoid only such dangers as are absolutely the immediate occasions of sin will most probably one day discover that he has fallen into grievous crimes and is lost. O God! with what attention are the great ones of this world

served! Everything is avoided that can possibly give them the least offense for fear of losing their favor; but with what carelessness are You served! Everything that can endanger the life of the body is shunned with the greatest caution, while the dangers which threaten the life of the soul are not feared!

O God! how negligently have I until now served You. Henceforth I will serve You with the greatest attention; be my helper and assist me.

2. O Christian brother! if God should act as sparingly with you as you do with him, what would become of you? If he should grant you only grace barely sufficient, would you be saved? You would be able to obtain [119] salvation, but you would not obtain it; because in this life temptations frequently occur so violent that it is morally impossible not to yield to them without a special assistance from God. But God does not give his special assistance to those who deal sparingly with him: *He who sows sparingly shall also reap sparingly.*1

But, O God! You have not dealt sparingly with me: while I have been so ungrateful towards You as to repay Your many favors with offenses, You, instead of chastising me, have redoubled Your graces towards me. No, my God! I will never more be ungrateful to You, as I have until now been.

3. To obtain salvation is not an easy task, but difficult, and very difficult. We carry about us the rebellious flesh, which allures to the gratification of sense; and we have, moreover, numberless enemies to contend with in the world, in hell, and within our own selves, who are ever tempting us to evil. It is true, the grace of God is never lacking to us; but still this grace requires us to struggle hard to overcome temptations, and to pray fervently to obtain more powerful assistance, as the danger becomes greater.

O Jesus! I desire nevermore to be separated from You and deprived of Your love. Until now I have been ungrateful to You, and have turned my back upon You, but will now love You with my whole soul, and fear nothing so much as to cease to love You. You know my weakness; assist me, therefore, You who are my only hope and confidence. And You, O ever-blessed Virgin Mary, cease not to intercede for me.

1 "Qui parce seminat, parce et metet." 2 Cor. 9.6.

MEDITATION 66.
The Appearance of the Body immediately after Death.

[120] 1. *Remember, man, that you are dust and into dust you shall return.***1** At present you can see, feel, speak, and move. The day will come when you will no longer see,

nor feel, nor speak, nor move. When your soul is separated from your body, your body will be consumed by worms and will moulder into dust; and your soul will go into eternity to be happy or miserable according as you have deserved by the actions of your life.

O God! I have deserved only Your displeasure and the punishments of hell; but You would not have me despair, but repent and love You, and place all my hopes in You.

2. Figure to yourself the body of one whose soul has just departed. Look on his corpse still remaining on the bed: the head fallen upon the chest, the hair in disorder and still bathed in the cold sweat of death, the eyes sunk, the cheeks fallen in, the face of the color of ashes, the lips and tongue black; so as to be loathsome and frightful to every beholder. See, dear Christian, to what a state your body will shortly be reduced which you now treat with so much indulgence.

O my God! I will no longer resist Your gracious calls. What now remains of the many gratifications with which I have indulged my body, but remorse of conscience which continually torments me? Oh that I had rather died than ever offended You!

3. When the body begins to corrupt, it becomes still more horrible. Twenty-four hours have scarcely elapsed

since that young person died, and already his corpse begins to be offensive. The windows of the apartment

1 "Memento, homo, quia pulvis es, et in pulverem reverteris." Gen. 3.19.

[121] must be opened, and perfumes employed, that the stench may not infect the whole house. His relatives and friends are in haste to commit him to the grave. He may have been a person of high rank, and to what does the pampering of his body now serve? It only hastens its corruption and increases its offensiveness.

Dearest Redeemer, although I knew that by sin I would greatly offend You, still I did commit it. To grant myself a short-lived satisfaction, I was willing to forfeit the invaluable treasures of Your grace. With sorrow do I cast myself prostrate at Your feet; pardon me through the blood which You have shed for me. Receive me again into Your favor, and chastise me as You please. I will willingly accept every chastisement, provided I be not deprived of Your love. I love You, O God! with my whole heart; I love You more than myself. Grant that I may remain faithful to You till the end of my life. Mary, my hope, intercede for me.

MEDITATION 67.
The State of the Body in the Grave.

1. Consider now, Christian brother, to what a state

your body will be reduced in the grave. It will first become livid and then black. Mould of a dirty white color will be produced over the whole surface of the flesh, from which a rotten fluid will begin to ooze and flow upon the ground. In this fluid a multitude of maggots will be generated, which will feast themselves upon the putrid flesh. Rats and other vermin will join in the feast and prey upon your poor carcass, some upon the outside, while others will enter into the mouth and others into the bowels. See to what a state that body will be reduced which for the sake of pleasure you have so often offended God.

[122] No, my God, I will never more offend You. Too many already have been my offenses. Enlighten me and strengthen me against temptations.

2. Then will your hair, cheeks, and lips fall off from your skull; your ribs will first be laid bare, and soon after your corrupted arms and legs. The worms, after having consumed all your flesh, will at last be consumed themselves. After this, nothing will remain of you but a mouldering skeleton, which in time will all fall to pieces; the head will be separated from the trunk, and the bones from one another. See then what man is, considered as a mortal being.

O Jesus! have pity on me. For how many years past have I deserved to burn in hell! I have forsaken You, my God, but You have not yet forsaken me. Pardon me, I beseech You, and permit me not anymore to abandon You; and when temptations assault me, may I ever have recourse to You.

3. Behold, finally, that bright young soldier who a little while ago was considered the life and soul of society; where is he now? Enter his house; he dwells there no longer. His bed is occupied by another, and others have already seized and divided his possessions. If you would see him, look into that newly made grave and you will behold a putrid mass of corruption, horrible and offensive. Saints of God, happy indeed are you, who, for the love of God, whom alone you loved in this world, were wise enough to mortify your bodies; now your bones are honored upon altars, and your souls happy in the enjoyment of God face to face. Your bodies at the last day will again be united with your souls, to be your companions in bliss as they were formerly your companions in suffering.

O God! I do not lament, but rejoice, that this my flesh, for which I have so often offended You, will one day be given to rottenness and worms: but I do indeed [123] lament the crimes I have committed against You, for You are infinite goodness. O Jesus! I love You, and will never, nevermore offend You. Mary, mother of God, pray for me.

MEDITATION 68.
Man is soon Forgotten after Death.

1. A young person has died early in life. A little while ago he was sought out for conversation, and everywhere welcomed by all; but now that he is dead, he has become the horror of those who behold him. His parents are in haste to get him out of the house, and call in bearers to carry him to the grave. How wretched if, to satisfy his parents or others of this world, he has lost God!

My dear Redeemer, though all may forget me, You will still remember me, for You have given Your life for my salvation. Oh that I had never offended You!

2. A little while ago the fame of his wit, gracefulness, refinement, and good humor was spread far and wide; but now that he is dead he is almost out of mind and will soon be quite forgotten. Upon hearing the news of his death, some may remark of him, "He did himself great credit;" others may exclaim, "Oh, how sad! What a clever, humorous, and delightful man he was!" Some may grieve for him because he was pleasant or useful to them; while others may perhaps rejoice, because his death may be of advantage to them; but in a short time no one will so much as mention him. Even his parents and nearest relatives do not like to hear him spoken of, that their grief for him may not be renewed; and from here in visits of condolence everything is made the sub-

ject of conversation but the person who is dead; and if any one begins to allude to him, he is immediately stopped with an exclamation, "Please do not mention him to me!" [124] See what becomes of the affection of our parents and friends for us in this world!

My God, I am content that You alone should love me, and will for the future love only You.

3. Your relatives will at first be afflicted at your death, but it will not be long before they will console themselves with the portion of your property which may fall to their lot; and in the same room in which your soul departed and was judged by Jesus Christ, they will feast, joke, dance, and laugh as before, and who knows where your soul will be?

Give me, O Lord, time to lament the offenses I have committed against You before You summon me to judgment! I will no longer resist Your calls : who knows but that this meditation may be the last call I may receive? I confess that I have deserved hell, and as many hells as I have committed mortal sins; but You will not despise poor penitent sinners. I am sincerely sorry with my whole soul for having abused Your infinite goodness by sensual gratifications. Forgive me and grant me grace to obey You and to love You till the end of my life. O Mary! I place myself under Your protection, and confide in Your holy intercession.

MEDITATION 69.
The Appearance of all Mankind in the Valley of Josaphat.

1. *The angels shall go out, and shall separate the wicked from among the just.*1 What would be the confusion of a person who, on entering into a church in the presence of a great concourse of people, would be forcibly expelled as one excommunicated! Alas! how much greater will the shame of the reprobate be to see themselves

1 "Exibunt angeli, et separabunt malos de medio justorum." Matt. 13.49.

[125] in the day of judgment expelled from the company of the saints in presence of all mankind! In this life the wicked are honored equally with the saints, and frequently more. But in that day, when the figure of this world passes away, the elect will be placed on the right hand, and caught up into the air to meet Jesus Christ, advancing to place crowns of glory on their heads, according to the words of the Apostle, *Then shall we be taken up together with them in the clouds to meet Christ in the air.*"1 But the wicked, surrounded by their tormentors, the infernal spirits, will be placed on the left hand, waiting for the appearance of the judge coming publicly to condemn them. O foolish worldlings! you who now hold the lives of the saints in derision and contempt, in the valley of Josaphat, you will change your sentiments. There will you acknowledge your folly, but it will be too late.

2. Oh, what a splendid appearance will the saints make on that day, who have forsaken all for God! How beautiful will be the appearance of the many young persons who, despising the riches and delights of the world, have shut themselves up in deserts or in cloisters, to attend only to their eternal salvation! And of the many martyrs who were so much despised and so cruelly tortured by the tyrants of this world! All these will be proclaimed courtiers of Jesus Christ in his heavenly glory. On the contrary, what a horrible appearance will a Herod make, or a Pilate, a Nero, or many others, who made so great a figure in this world, but died under God's displeasure!

Jesus, I embrace Your holy cross. What are riches, what are honors, what is the whole world? Besides You, what do I desire?

3. Christian, what will be your station at the last day?

1 "Rapiemur cum illis in nubibus obviam Christo in aera." 1 Thes. 4.16.

[126] The right hand or the left? If you would occupy the right, you must walk in the way which conducts there; it is impossible to keep the way to the left, and at length arrive at the right.

O Lamb of God! who came into the world to take away our sins, have pity on me. I am sorry for having offended You, and will love You above all things; permit me not to offend You any more. I seek not worldly goods; give me only Your grace and Your love, and I ask for nothing more. O Mary, You are my refuge and my hope.

MEDITATION 70.
The Blindness of those who say, If we be lost we shall not be lost alone.

1. What do you say? that if you go to hell you will not go alone? But what consolation will the company of the wicked be to you in hell? Every condemned soul in hell weeps and laments, saying, Although I am condemned to suffer forever, would that I might suffer alone! The wretched company which you will meet with there will increase your torments by their despairing groans and moanings. What a torment to hear even a dog howling all night long, or an infant crying for five or six hours, and not to be able to sleep! And what will it be to hear the yells and howlings of so many wretched souls in despair, who will continually torment one another with their dismal noises, and this, not for one night, nor for many nights only, but for all eternity!

2. Again, your companions will but increase the torments of hell, by the stench of their burning carcasses. *Out of their carcasses*, says the prophet Isaiah, *shall a stench arise.***1** They are called carcasses, not because they are dead, for they are alive to pain, but because of the

1 "De cadaveribus eorum ascendet foetor." Isaiah 34.3.

[127] stench which they will emit. Your companions will also increase the torments of hell by their numbers; they will be in that pit as grapes in the wine-press of the anger of God: *He treads,* said St. John, *the wine-press of the fierceness of the wrath of God the Almighty.***1** They will be pressed on every side, so as to be unable to move hand or foot so long as God shall be God.

3. O accursed sin! how can you so blind men who are gifted with reason? Sinners, who pretend to despise damnation, are yet more careful to preserve their goods, their situations, and their health; they do not say, "If I lose my property, my place, my health, I shall not be the only one who will lose such things." Yet when the soul is at stake, they say, "If I be lost, I shall not be lost alone!" He who loses the good things of this world and saves his soul will find a recompense for all he has lost; but he who loses his soul, what compensation will he find? *What shall he give in exchange for his soul?***2**

O my God, enlighten me and do not forsake me. How often have I sold my soul to the devil, and exchanged Your grace and favor for a wretched transitory indulgence of sense! I am sorry, O God! for having thus dishonored Your infinite majesty. My God, I love You: permit me not to lose You any more. O Mary, Mother of God! deliver me from hell, and from the guilt of sin by Your holy intercession.

MEDITATION 71.
The Measure of Grace.

1. There is a certain measure beyond which God does
not bestow his graces upon us. We should therefore be
very much afraid of abusing any of the graces which

1 "Et ipse calcat torcular vini furoris irae Dei." Rev. 19.15.
2 "Quam dabit homo commutationem pro anima sua?" Matt. 16.26.

[128] our Lord dispenses to us. Every grace, every light,
every call, may be the last we shall receive from God,
and by despising it we may lose our souls.

O my God! You have already bestowed too many
graces upon me, and too often have I abused them.
Have mercy on me, and do not yet abandon me.
2. This measure is not the same for all persons; but
for some greater, for others less. Christian brother,
think how many graces you have received from God;
and if you continue to abuse them, will you be saved?
Reflect that the more abundant the graces have been
which God has granted you, the more should you fear
lest he abandon you in your sins, and the more should
you be resolved upon a change of life. It may be that
by one more mortal sin you may close against you the

gates of mercy, and ruin your soul forever. And it may not be so. But you should very much fear lest it should be so. And truly miserable you are if you do not thus fear.

No, my God, I desire nevermore to lose You. Whenever the devil shall tempt me, I will have recourse to You, my Jesus; I know that You are ever ready to assist those who fly to You for help.

3. The greater the graces, the greater is the ingratitude of him who abuses them. The graces which you have received should induce you to hope that the Lord will pardon you if you amend your life and remain faithful to him for the future. But they should also make you fear lest God should condemn you to hell, if after so many offenses you continue still to provoke him by sin. O God! I give You thanks for not having even yet forsaken me. The light which You at present impart to me, the displeasure which I feel for having offended You, the desire which I have to love You and to continue in Your grace, are certain signs that You have not yet abandoned me. And since You have not abandoned me after so many sins, I desire nevermore to [129] abandon You, who are the God of my soul. I love You above all things; and because I love You, I am sorry for having despised You. Through Your sacred Passion I beseech You, O Jesus! to grant me perseverance. Holy Mary, queen of mercy, take me under Your protection.

MEDITATION 72.
Loving God because He has Died for us.

1. *He loved me,* says the Apostle, *and delivered Himself for me.***1** When was a master ever known to lay down his life for the love of his servant? or a king for the love of his slave? And yet it is certainly true that my Creator, the Lord of heaven and earth, the Son of God, has of his own will laid down his life for the love of me his vile and ungrateful creature. St. Bernard says, "He spared not himself that he might spare his servant."**2** To pardon me, he would not pardon himself, but condemned himself to die in torments upon a cross.

I believe, O Jesus! that You have died for me, and how has it been possible for me to have lived so many years without loving You?

2. But, my Redeemer, You have given Your life not only for a vile creature, but for a rebellious and ungrateful creature, who has oftentimes turned his back upon You, and for some base gratification renounced Your grace and Your love. You have sought by the most endearing motives to make me love You; and I have sought to make You hate me and condemn me to hell. Nevertheless, that same love which induced You to die for me, now induces me to hope that You will not reject me if I return to You. Pardon me, O Jesus!

1 "Dilexit me, et tradidit semetipsum pro me." Gal. 2.20.
2 "Ut servum redimeret, sibi Filius ipse non pepercit." *Sermon on the Passion of the Lord.*

[130] I am sensible of the wrong which I have done You; and I know also the wrong I should still do You, were I to love You only in a slight degree: no, I will love You to the utmost of my power; too much have You deserved such a love. Grant me Your help and assistance.

3, Ah, my Savior, what more could You have done to gain my heart than You have done by dying for my sake? What greater love could You have shown for Your friend than to die for the love of him? *Greater love than this no man has, that a man lay down his life for his friends.***1** Since then, O Word incarnate, You can do nothing more to make me love You, shall I continue to be ungrateful to You? No, death is approaching, and is perhaps very near me, and I will not die so ungrateful to You as I until now have been. I love You, my beloved Jesus. You have given Yourself entirely to me; I will give myself entirely to You. Bind and straighten me with the bonds of Your love, so that I may live and die in the love of Your infinite goodness. O sacred Mother Mary! take me under Your protection, and teach me to burn with the love of Your divine Son, who died on the cross for the love of me.

MEDITATION 73.
The Care of our Salvation.

1. The devil makes salvation appear to some too
difficult to be accomplished, in order to dishearten them
and induce them to abandon themselves to a disorderly
life. It is true that if to obtain salvation it were necessary to retire into a desert, or to shut one's self up in a
cloister, we ought to do so. But these extraordinary
means are not necessary; ordinary means are sufficient,

1 "Majorem hac dilectionem nemo habet, ut animam suam ponat
quis pro amicis suis." John 15.13.

[131] such as the frequenting of the sacraments, the avoiding of dangerous occasions [of sin], and the frequently
recommending of ourselves by prayer to God. At our death
we shall see that these things were easy; from here will our
remorse be very great if until then we have neglected them.
2. We should resolve and say, "I will save my soul,
cost what it may." All other things may perish - property,
friends, and even life itself if I can but only save my
soul! Let us never think we can do too much to obtain
eternal salvation. Eternity is at stake, the being happy
or miserable forever. *"No security can be too great,"*
says St. Bernard, *"where eternity is at stake."***1**

O God! I am ashamed to appear before You; how
often for a mere nothing have I turned my back upon
You! No, I will never more forfeit Your grace, nor

willfully become Your enemy. *In You, O Lord, have I hoped; let me not be confounded forever.*2 I would rather a thousand times lose my life than lose Your friendship.

3. If during the past we have forfeited salvation, we must now endeavor to remedy the evil; we must change our lives, and this without delay. It is to no purpose to say I will do so in a short time. Hell is filled with souls who formerly said the same; but death surprised them, and prevented their fulfillment. What a favor would God bestow upon a dying man on the point of breathing his last, were he to grant him one more year, or even one more month! Christian brother, at this very time, God bestows such a favor upon you, and what use do you make of it?

Why, O God, do I delay? Do I wait for the period when there will be no more time for me, and when I shall find that I have in reality done nothing for You? I have the consolation of being as yet assisted by Your

1 Nulla nimia securitas, ubi periclitatur aeternitas.
2 "In te, Domine, speravi; non confundar in aeternum." Ps. 30.2.

[132] grace. I love You above every good, and desire rather to die than to offend You. But You know my weakness, and the many treasons I have been guilty of against You. Help me, O Jesus! in You do I place all my hopes; and to You, O Mary, Mother of God, do I

fly for protection.

MEDITATION 74.
The Leaving of All at Death.

1. Christians are well aware that they must die, yet
for the most part they live as though they were never to
die. If after this life there were no other life, if there
were neither hell nor heaven, could they think less of
death than they now do? If, dear Christian, you desire
to live well, endeavor to spend the remainder of your
days in the continual remembrance of death. Oh, how
correctly does he judge of things, and how rightly does
he direct all his actions, who performs them with a view
to his departure from here! The remembrance of death
destroys in him all affection for the good things of this
world, by reminding him that he must soon leave them
all behind him.

O God! since You give me time to remedy the evil
which I have done, make known to me Your will, and I
will do all that You require of me.

2. If a traveler, on his journey to his own country,
were to stop and spend all he has in building a palace in a
land through which he ought only to pass, and neglect to
provide a dwelling for himself in that country in which he
was to reside his whole life, he would be thought mad.

And must not the Christian be deemed mad who thinks only of gratifying himself in this world, through which he has only to pass during a few days, and heeds not the danger of being miserable in the next, where he must live forever, as long as God shall be God?

[133] Woe to me, O God! If you had called me out of life in my sins! I thank You for having borne with me with such great patience. Never permit me to be again separated from You. My God, my sovereign good, I do and will love You above all things.

3. Death will rob us of all things. Whatever we may have acquired in this world we must leave all behind us at our death. Nothing will then be allowed us but a coffin and a shroud, which will soon moulder away and become dust with our bodies. We must then leave the house which we now inhabit, and a dismal grave must be the dwelling-place of our bodies until the day of judgment, when they must go either to heaven or to hell, accordingly as our souls have gone before them. All things will therefore end with me in death. Then shall I find that nothing will remain for me but the little which I have done for God. And were I to die this moment, what should I find that I have done for You, my Jesus? For what do I delay? that death may come and find me thus miserable? No, my God, I will amend my life. I detest all the offenses I have ever committed against You. For the future I will not seek to gratify

my own inclinations, but solely to do Your will, who are the God of my soul. I love You, O infinite goodness! I love You above all things; mercifully grant me Your grace. And do You also, Mary, Mother of God, pray to Your divine Son for me.

MEDITATION 75.
The Moment of Death.

1. Imagine yourself, dear Christian, just now dead, and your soul entered into eternity. If now you have just departed from this world, what would you not wish to have done for life eternal? But what would such [134] wishes avail you, If you had not spent the days of your mortal life in serving God? If you would now prevent that which you have time to prevent, place yourself in imagination frequently for the future in your grave, or rather upon your death-bed; imagine yourself to be dying, on the point of breathing your last, listen to the reproaches of your conscience and delay not to silence them by repentance. Delay not, for you have no time to lose.

Ah, my God! enlighten me, make known to me the way in which I should walk, and I will obey You in all things.

2. St. Camillus de Lellis, looking at the graves of the

dead, was accustomed to say, *"If those who are here interred could now return to life again, what would they not do to become saints! And I who have time at my disposal, what do I do for God?"* Thus did this saint animate himself to become more and more closely united with his Lord. Know then, dear Christian, that the time which God in his mercy now grants you is of the greatest value. Do not wait for time to labor for your salvation until you are gone into eternity, or until the arrival of that awful moment when it will be said to you, *"Depart, Christian soul, out of this world;"* make haste to go forth, for there is no more time for you to labor: what is done is done.

O Jesus! remember that I am the lost sheep for which You have laid down Your life. "We beseech You, therefore, help Your servants, whom You have redeemed with Your precious blood." Give me light and grace to do that now which I shall wish to have done at the hour of my death.

3. O eternal God! I tremble at the thought of being that unhappy tree of which You have said: *Behold for these three years I come seeking fruit on this fig tree, and I find none. Cut it down therefore: why does it encumber* [135] *the ground?*1 Yet so it is, O Lord! for the many years I have now lived upon this earth, what good have I until now done? What fruit have I brought You all this time, but sin and bitterness? Alas! how have I deserved

to have dwelt long ago in hell! Dearest Redeemer, spare me yet a little longer; I will not be obstinate; death will never find me in the state in which I now am. I will deplore and detest the days which I have spent in offending You, and will pass the remainder of my life in loving and honoring Your infinite goodness. I do and will love You, my sovereign good. Take not Your help away from me. And You, O Blessed Virgin Mary, deprive me not of Your powerful protection.

MEDITATION 76.
The Examination of our Sins at the Last Day.

1. Behold the heavens will open, and the angels and saints will descend to be present at the judgment followed by the Queen of Heaven, the ever blessed Virgin, and after her will appear the eternal Judge of the living and of the dead, encompassed with great power and majesty. The appearance of Jesus will be to the just the greatest consolation; but to the wicked, the indignant countenance of the Son of God will be horror and confusion worse than hell itself. *They will say to the mountains : Fall upon us, and hide us from the wrath of the Lamb.* 2 They will desire that the mountains may immediately fall upon them rather than behold the indignant countenance of the Lamb, that is, of the Redeemer, who in their lifetime was as a lamb

1 "Ecce, anni tres sunt, ex quo venio quaerens fructum in ficulnea hac, et non invenio." Luke 13.7.
2 "Dicunt montibus et petris: Cadite super nos, et abscondite nos a facie sedentis super thronum et ab ira Agni." Rev. 6.16.

[136] towards them, in silently bearing with their re- peated injuries against him.

O Jesus! You who will one day be my Judge; I am heartily sorry for having so grievously offended You. Pardon me my sins, and grant that when You appear as my Judge, I may not behold You indignant against me.

2. *The judgment sat, and the books were opened.*1 Then will it be impossible to conceal our sins; Jesus himself, who will be our Judge, having long ago witnessed them, will manifest them to the whole world. *He will bring to light the hidden things of darkness.*2 Even the most secret sins, the most abominable impurities, and cruelties the most horrible, he will make known to all mankind.

O my Redeemer! You who already know all my iniquities, have mercy on me now, before the time of mercy ends.

3. In a word, Jesus Christ will on that day make him self known as the great Lord of all : *The Lord shall be known*, says the Psalmist, *when he executes judgment.*3 At present more account is made of some pleasure, of a mere

vapor, of a fit of passion, than of God. Hence will
the Judge then justly say to the sinner, *To whom have you
likened me, or made me equal?***4** To what have you com-
pared me and postponed me? Have your base inclinations, or a mere caprice, prevailed with you more than
my grace? O God! what shall we then answer to such
reproaches? Oh, how will our utter confusion close our
mouths! But let us now answer and say:

O Jesus! I know that You will one day be my Judge,
but now You are my Savior. Remember that You
have died for me. I am sorry with my whole heart for

1 "Judicium sedit, et libri aperti sunt." Dan. 7.10.
2 "Illuminabit abscondita tenebrarum." 1 Cor. 4.5.
3 "Cognoscetur Dominus judicia faciens." Ps. 9.17.
4 "Cui assimilastis me? . . . dicit Sanctus." Isaiah 40.25.

[137] having despised You, my sovereign good. But if
until now I have despised You, behold I now esteem and
love You more than myself, and am willing to die for Your
love. O Jesus! pardon me, and never permit me to live any
more deprived of Your love. Mary, most gracious advocate
of sinners, help me now while I can yet receive your power
ful assistance.

MEDITATION 77.
The Great Love of God for our Souls.

1. The love which God bears our souls is eternal and
infinite. *I have loved You with an everlasting love.***1** So
that God has from all eternity loved every human soul.
For the salvation of souls he placed all other creatures in
the world: *All things for the sake of the elect.***2** And lastly
he sent his only Son into the world, made man for our
sake, to die upon the cross for the salvation of our souls.

You, O God! have indeed loved me from all eternity,
and have died for me, and how could I ever so grievously
offend You?

2. The only begotten Son of God, for the love of our
souls, came down from heaven to free them from eternal
death by his own death upon the cross; and having redeemed them with his blood, he called his angels to
rejoice with him for the recovery of his lost sheep:
*Rejoice with Me, because I have found the sheep that
was lost.***3**

Dearest Redeemer, You came to seek me, and how have
I until now fled away from You. No, my Jesus! I will no
more fly from You. I will love You; and oh! do You so
bind me to You by Your holy love that I may live and
die in Your sacred embraces.

1 "In charitate perpetua dilexi te." Jer. 31.3.
2 "Omnia . . . propter electos." 2 Tim. 2.10.
3 "Congratulamini mihi, quia inveni ovem meam quae perierat.
Luke 15.6.

[138] 3. The eternal Father has then given his Son, and the divine Son has given his precious blood and life for the salvation of my soul; and how often have I withdrawn myself from God and sold myself for something worse than nothing to his and my mortal enemy the devil!

Truly, my God! You have spared nothing to save me from being lost, while I, for the sake of some paltry gratification, have many, many times renounced Your friendship and love. You have borne with me, that I might have time to bewail my sins and to love You, the God of my soul. I will therefore love You, my only good, and will grieve above every evil for having so often offended You. Oh! permit me not to be anymore separated from Your love. Remind me continually how much You have done for my salvation, and how great has been the love which You have shown me, that I may never cease to love You, my treasure, my life, and my all. Grant that I may ever love You, and then dispose of me as You please. Mary, Mother of God, Your divine Son denies You nothing; recommend to him, I beseech You, my sinful soul.

MEDITATION 78.
The Remorse of the Reprobate.

1. The condemned soul is tormented with three kinds of remorse. The first arises from reflecting for what a mere trifle it has incurred everlasting misery. For how long does the pleasure of sin last? only for a moment. To a man at the point of death, how long does his past life appear? a mere moment. But to one in hell, what do the fifty or sixty years of his sojourning upon the earth appear, v/hen, in the gulf of eternity, he foresees that after a hundred or a thousand millions of years he will be only beginning eternity? Alas! does he exclaim, for a few moments of indulgence in poisonous pleasures, [139] which I did but just taste, I must forever suffer, lament, and despair in this fiery furnace, abandoned by all, as long as God shall be God.

O my God! I give You thanks for Your great mercy to me, and implore You still to have mercy on me.

2. The second kind of remorse arises from the reflection of the condemned soul on the little which it need have done to be saved, but did not do it; and that now there is no remedy. Alas! does it say, if I have frequently confessed my sins, given myself to prayer, restored that ill-gotten property, pardoned my enemies, avoided that dangerous occasion, I should not have been lost. What would it have cost me? Although it might

have cost me much, yet I ought to have been most will
ing to do my utmost to be saved. But I did not do it,
and now I am lost forever. With how many inspirations
did God favor me! How many times did he call me
and admonish me that unless I desisted I should certainly be lost! I might then have remedied my past
iniquity, but now I have no remedy. Ah! how does
this thought afflict the wretched soul, even more than
the fire and all the other torments of hell, that it might
have been happy forever, but now must be miserable for
all eternity!

O Jesus! it is now the time of mercy; do You mercifully pardon me. I love You, my sovereign good, and
am exceedingly sorry for having ever despised You.

3. The third and most bitter kind of remorse arises
from the consciousness of the wretched soul of the great
happiness which it has forfeited through its own fault. It
recollects that God afforded it abundant means of gaining
heaven, that he died for its salvation, permitted it to be
born in the bosom of the true Church, and bestowed
upon it numberless graces, and it reflects that all have
been rendered useless through its own fault. I am lost,
it exclaims, and neither the merits of Jesus Christ, nor
[140] the intercession of the Mother of God, nor the
prayers of the saints, are of any avail to me; every
gleam of hope is vanished from me forever.

Oh that I had died, my God, rather than ever offended You! Receive me now into Your favor; I love You, and will love You forever. Mary, most gracious advocate of sinners, intercede for me.

MEDITATION 79.
Jesus, the King of Love.

1. St. Fulgentius, contemplating the Infant Jesus fly ing into Egypt from the hands of Herod, who through fear of losing his kingdom sought the infant's life, tenderly exclaims, "Why are You thus troubled, O Herod? The King who is just now born comes not to over throw other kings by force of arms, but to subjugate them by dying for them."**1** As though he have said, The King of heaven is not come to conquer us by war, but by love; he is not come to put us to death, but to rescue us from death by dying for us. Hence it is that Jesus may indeed be styled the King of love.

Oh that I had always loved You, O Jesus, my sovereign King! and have never offended You! You did spend thirty-three years in pain and labor to save me from being lost, and I have willfully renounced You, my sovereign good, for the sake of momentary pleasures. Father of mercy, forgive me, and embrace me with the kiss of peace.

2. Ungrateful Jews! why did you refuse to acknowledge for your king one so lovely and so loving towards
you? Why did you exclaim, *We have no king but Caesar*?**2**

1 "Quid est quod sic turbaris, Herodes? Rex iste qui natus est, non
venit reges pugnando superare, sed moriendo subjugare." *S. de
Epiph. et Inn. nece.*
2 "Non habemus regem nisi Caesarem." John 19.15.

[141] Caesar did not love you, nor desire to die for you;
while your true King have descended from heaven upon
the earth to die for the love of you.

Sweet Savior! if others will not receive You as their King,
I will have no other King but You: "You are my King."**1**
I know that You alone love me; You alone have redeemed
me with Your blood; where then shall I find one who has
loved me as You have loved me? I am grieved for having
until now rejected You as my King, by losing my respect
for You and rebelling against You. Pardon me, O Jesus,
my King! for You have died to purchase pardon for me.

3. To this end Christ died and arose again j that he might
be Lord of the dead and of the living.**2**

My beloved King, dearest Jesus, since You earnest
upon earth to gain our hearts to Yourself, if until now I
have resisted Your loving calls, I will now no longer
resist them. Do not disdain to receive me; I now give
myself to You, I give You my whole self. Take, O

King! possession of my whole will, and of my whole self; make me faithful to You; and grant that I may rather die than betray You any more, my King, my love and only good. O Queen, and Mother of my King! O Mary, obtain for me that fidelity which I this day promise to Your divine Son.

MEDITATION 80.
The Miserable Death of the Sinner.

1. Poor unhappy being! see how he is oppressed with sorrows! Alas! he is now about to die; a cold sweat is stealing over him, his breath is failing him, and he frequently faints away; and when come to himself, his

1 Rex meus es tu.
2 "In hoc enim Christus mortuus est et resurrexit, ut et mortuorum et vivorum dominetur." Rom. 14.9.

[142] head is so far gone and so weak that he can attend but to very little, understand but little, and speak but little. But the worst is, although he is drawing near his end, instead of thinking of the account he must shortly render to God, he thinks only of his medical attendants, and of the remedies they may be able to allow him to save him from death. And those who stand around him, instead of exhorting him to unite himself to God, flatter him by telling him that he is better, or say not a word, that they may not disturb him.

O my God! deliver me from such an unhappy end.

2. But at last the priest admonishes him of his approaching dissolution, saying to him, "You are now, dear brother, in a state of great danger, and must bid farewell to the world; give yourself then to God, and receive his holy sacraments." On hearing this fatal announcement, how dreadfully is he agitated, what sadness and remorse of conscience overwhelm him, and how dreadful is the conflict which he suffers! All the sins he has committed appear in confusion before him, the inspirations which he has neglected, his broken promises, and the many years of his past life now lost and gone forever, all rush upon his mind. He now opens his eyes to the truths of eternity, of which during his past life he made but very little account. O God! what terror do the thoughts of loss of Your favor, of death, of judgment, of hell, and of eternity, strike into his unhappy soul!

O Jesus! have pity on me and pardon me; do not abandon me. I am sensible of the evil I have done in despising You, and would willingly die for Your love. Assist me, O God! to begin now at least a new life.
3. The dying sinner exclaims, "O what great folly have I been guilty of! How have I squandered away my life! I might have been a saint, and I would not; and now, what can I do? My head wanders, and fears oppress me and will not permit me to bring my mind [143] to any one good work! In a few moments what

will become of me? Dying in this manner, how can I be saved?" He wishes for time to make his peace effectually with God, but time is no longer his. "Alas!" he cries out, "this cold sweat is a sure symptom of the near approach of death; I begin to lose my sight and my breath; I can no longer move, I can hardly speak." And thus, in the midst of so much confusion, despondency, and fear, his soul departs from his body and appears before Jesus Christ.

O my Jesus! Your death is my hope. I love You above every good, and because I love You, I am sorry for having offended You. Mary, Mother of God, pray to Jesus for me.

MEDITATION 81.
The Happy Death of the Just.

1. To the just man death is not a punishment, but a reward; it is not dreaded by him, but desired. How can it be dreadful to him if it is to terminate all his pains, afflictions, and conflicts, and all danger of losing God? Those words, "Depart, Christian soul, out of this world,"[1] which strike such terror into the soul of the sinner, fill the soul that loves God with joy. The just man is not afflicted at leaving the good things of this world, because God has always been his only good; not at leaving honors, because he has always regarded them as

smoke; not at being separated from his friends and relatives, because he has always loved them in God and for God. Hence, as in life he frequently exclaimed, "My God and my all!" he now repeats the same in death, with ecstasies of delight; the time being at hand for him to return to his God who made him, to love him face to face forever and ever in heaven.

1 Proficiscere, anima Christiana, de hoc mundo.

[144] 2. The sorrows of death do not afflict him; he even rejoices to sacrifice the last remnants of his life as a testimony of his love for God, uniting the sufferings of his death to the sufferings of Jesus when dying on the cross. The thought that the time of sin and the danger of losing God are now past overwhelms him with delight. The devil fails not to suggest to his mind thoughts of despondency at the recollection of his past sins; but as he has for many years bewailed them, and loved Jesus Christ with his whole heart, he is not dismayed, but comforted.

O Jesus! how good and faithful are You to a soul that seeks and loves You!

3. As the sinner who dies in mortal sin experiences, in the internal troubles and rage which he suffers in death, a foretaste of hell; so does the just man experience in death a foretaste of heaven. His acts of confidence and

of the love of God, and his ardent desire to see God, allow him a beginning of that happiness which is soon to be completed for him in heaven. With what gladness does he welcome the holy Viaticum when brought into his chamber! He exclaims like St. Philip Neri when he was on his death-bed, "Because I have offended You, my God, I will say to You, with St. Bernard, Your wounds are my merits.

O my God! if I am in Your grace, as I hope I am, grant me soon to die, that I may presently behold and love You face to face, and be secure of nevermore losing You. Mary, my Mother, obtain for me a holy death.

MEDITATION 82.
At the Point of Death.

1. If now you were at the point of death, already in your agony and almost breathing your last, and about to appear before the divine tribunal, what would you [145] not wish to have done for God? And what would you not give for a little more time to make your salvation more secure? Woe to me, if I do not make use of the light that is now given me, and amend my life! *He has called against me the time.*1 The time which is now granted me by the mercy of God will be a great torment and a subject of bitter remorse to me at the hour of

death, when time for me will be no more.

O Jesus! You did spend Your whole life for my salvation, and I have been many years in the world, and
yet what have I until now done for You? Alas! all that
I have done gives me only pain and remorse of conscience.

2. Christian, God now gives You time, be then resolved: in what will you spend it? What do you wait
for? Do you wait to see that light which will show you
your wretched neglect, when there will be no remedy?
Do you wait to hear that "Go forth" which must be
obeyed without demur?

O my God! I will no longer abuse the light which
You afford me; but which I have until now so much
abused. I thank You for this fresh admonition, which,
may be the last You will ever give me. But since at
present You thus enlighten me, it is a mark that
You have not yet abandoned me, and are desirous of
showing me mercy. My beloved Savior, I am sorry
above all things for having so often despised Your
graces and neglected Your calls and inspirations. I
promise with Your help never more to offend You.

3. O God! how many Christians die in the greatest
uncertainty as to their salvation, and tormented with the
thought that they have have time to serve You, and are

now arrived at the end of their life, when no more time is left them for any good works! They are sensible that now all that remains to them is to render a strict account

1 "Vocavit adversum me tempus." Lam. 1.15.

[146] of the many graces and inspirations bestowed upon them by God, and know not what to answer.

O Lord! I will not die under such a torment. Say what You require of me, make known to me the way of life in which I should walk, and I will obey You in all things. Until now I have despised Your commands, but I am now sorry for it with my whole heart, and love You above all things. O Mary, refuge of sinners! recommend my soul to Your divine Son.

MEDITATION 83.
The Rashness of the Sinner in Committing Mortal Sin.

1. God cannot but hate mortal sin, because mortal sin is directly opposed to his divine will: "Sin," says St. Bernard, "would destroy the divine will."**1** As he can not but hate mortal sin, so he cannot but hate the sinner who identifies himself with sin and rebels against his God: *To God the wicked and his wickedness are hateful alike.***2** How great then is the rashness of the sinner in committing sin, when he knows that by so doing he

will bring upon himself the hatred of God!

my God! have mercy on me; You have distinguished
me with many graces, and I have repaid You with nu-
merous offenses; no one has so grievously offended
You as I have done. Grant me, for Your mercy's sake,
contrition for my sins.

2. God is that all-powerful being who by a single act of
his will created all things: *He commanded and they were
made.***3** And he can in like manner, by a single act of his
will, destroy all that he has created, whenever he pleases:

1 Peccatum est destructivum divinae voluntatis.
2 "Similiter autem odio sunt Deo impius et impietas ejus." Wis. 14.9.
3 "Quoniam ipse dixit, et facta sunt." Ps. 32.9.

[147] *With a word he can utterly destroy the whole world.***1**
And will the sinner have the hardihood to put himself in op-
position to this omnipotent God and make him his enemy?
He has stretched out his hand, says holy Job, *against God,
and has strengthened himself against the Almighty.***2** What
should we think of an ant pretending to fight against an
armed soldier?

And what ought to be said of me, O eternal God! who
have so often dared to oppose myself to You, making
no account of Your power, and sensible that I was drawing down Your anger upon me? But Your holy Passion,
Jesus, gives me confidence to hope in You for pardon,

who did die to obtain forgiveness for me.

3. The rashness of the sinner increases when we reflect
that he offends God before his own eyes: *He provokes
Me to anger before My face.*3 What subjects have ever
the audacity to break the laws in the presence of the king
himself? But the sinner knows that God beholds him,
and yet he does not hesitate to commit sin before him.

My dear Redeemer, I am that audacious being who
has dared to despise Your holy precepts before Your face.

I have therefore deserved hell; but You are my Savior,
who yearns to take away the sins of the world and to
save poor sinners: *The Son of man is come to seek and to
save that which was lost.*4 How much am I grieved for
having offended You! You have given me many
proofs of Your love, and I have returned You as many
injuries. O Jesus! put an end to my sins, and replenish
me with Your love. I love You, O infinite love! and

1 "Potest . . . et universum mundum uno nutu delere." 2 Mach. 8.18.
2 "Tetendit enim adversus Deum manum suam, et contra Omnipotentem
roboratus est." Job 15.25.
3 "Ad iracundiam provocat me ante faciem meam semper." Isaiah 65.3.
4 "Venit enim Films hominis quaerere et salvum facere quod perierat."
Luke 19.10.

[148] tremble at the thought of being ever again deprived
of Your love, Permit it not, O God! rather let me die. O
Mary, You obtain whatever You ask of God; obtain for me

the gift of holy perseverance.

MEDITATION 84.
The Parable of the Prodigal Son.

1. St. Luke writes (chap. 15) that an ungrateful son, disdaining to remain in subjection to his father, went one day to demand from him his inheritance, that he might live as he pleased; and having obtained it, turned his back upon his father and went his way to live in vice in a far distant country, This prodigal son is a figure of the sinner, who, abusing the liberty which God has granted him, forsakes God, and lives in iniquity far away from him.

O my Lord, and my Father! this is what I have done, when to satisfy my capricious desires I have so often forsaken You, to live at a distance from You deprived of Your grace.

2. But as it happened to the prodigal son, that, having left his father, he was reduced to so great misery that he was unable to satisfy himself with the husks which the swine refused to eat; so does it happen to the sinner. When he forsakes God, he can nowhere find contentment nor peace; because, at a distance from God, all the pleasures of the earth cannot satisfy his heart. The prodigal son, seeing himself reduced to such a state

of misery, said within himself, *I will arise and go to my father.*1 Do You, Christian, in like manner, arise from the filth of sin and return to your heavenly Father, who will not reject you.

Yes, my God, my Father, I confess that I have done evil in forsaking You; I am sorry for it and repent of

1 Surgam, et ibo ad patrem meum. Lk. 15.18.

[149] it with my whole heart. Oh, do not cast me off now that I return to You penitent, and resolved nevermore to depart from before Your feet. My dear Father, forgive me, pardon me, give me the kiss of peace and receive me into Your favor.

3. The prodigal son, on his return, cast himself with humility at his father's feet and said, *Father, I am not worthy to be called Your son.*1 Upon which his father embraced him with tenderness, and, forgetting all his past ingratitude, welcomed him with the greatest affection, and was overjoyed at regaining his son who was lost.

Most tender Father, permit me to cast myself with sorrow at Your feet, for my multiplied offenses against You. I am not worthy to be called Your son, having so many times forsaken and despised You; but I know that You are so good a parent that You will not reject a repentant child. If until now I have not loved You, I will now love You above all things, and will willingly undergo any suffering for Your love. Assist me with Your holy grace, that I may ever remain faithful to You. O Mary, God is my Father, You are my Mother; be not forgetful of me.

MEDITATION 85.
The Evil of Lukewarmness.

1. Great indeed is the evil which tepidity occasions in the souls of those who, while they have a dread of being in a state of mortal sin, make but little account of deliberate venial sins, and take no pains to avoid them. God threatens the lukewarm to vomit them out of his mouth: *Because You are lukewarm I will begin to vomit You out of My mouth.*2 This means rejection on the part of God; and what is once rejected, in the way here men-

1 Pater, . . . jam non sum dignus vocari filius tuus.
2. "Quia tepidus es . . . incipiam te evomere." Rev. 3.16.

[150] tioned, is never received again. The tepid Christian dishonors God, by showing in his conduct that he does not consider God deserving of being served with the greatest attention.
Yes, my God! I have indeed until now dishonored You in this manner, but I will now amend my life; do help and support me.

2. St. Teresa never fell into any grievous sin, as is related in the Bull of her canonization; yet it was revealed to her that a place was prepared for her in hell, if she did not shake off her tepidity. How was this, since it is only mortal sin that is punished in hell? The Holy Spirit supplies the answer, when he says, *He that despises small things shall fall by little and little.***1** He who makes no account of deliberate venial sins will easily fall into "those which are mortal; because by habitually offending Almighty God in small things he will not have much dread of sometimes offending him in great things; and because by continually withdrawing himself from God, he provokes God not to grant him those special helps without which he will easily be overcome by powerful temptations.

Abandon me not, O Lord, to such a misfortune; grant that I may rather die; have pity on me.

3. *He who sows sparingly, shall also reap sparingly.***2** With justice does God withhold his graces from the soul that loves and serves him slothfully. Hence says the prophet, *Cursed is he who does the work of God deceitfully.***3** He therefore who serves God deceitfully, must commit a great evil, since God curses him. The grievous sinner, conscious of his crimes, confesses them; but the tepid Christian, deeming himself to be better than others be-

1 "Qui spernit modica, paulatim decidet." Eccles. 19.1.

2 "Qui parce seminat, parce et metet." 2 Cor. 9.6.
3 "Maledictus qui facit opus Dei fraudulenter." Jer. 48.10.

[151] cause he is not guilty of great sins, lives on in the mire of his defects, and does not humble himself.

O my God! I have by my tepidity closed up the avenue of those graces which You were willing to be stow upon me. Help me, O Lord! for I am resolved to amend my life. There is no reason why I should be sparing with You, who have given Your life for me. Holy Mary, Mother of God, help me; in Your patronage I confide.

MEDITATION 86.
The Giving of Ourselves to God without Reserve.

1. God has declared that he loves all those who love him: *I love them that love Me.*1 But it is not to be supposed that God will give himself entirely to one who loves anything in the world equally with God. At one time St. Teresa was in this state, keeping up an affection, not indeed an impure affection, but an inordinate one, for a certain relative. When, however, she divested herself of this attachment, God was pleased to say to her in a vision, "Now that You are wholly mine, I am wholly thine."

O my God! when will the day arrive when I shall be wholly Yours? Consume within me, I beseech You,

by the flames of Your divine love, all those earthly affec-
tions which hinder me from belonging entirely to You.
When shall I be able to say to You with truth, My God,
You only do I desire, and besides You there is nothing that
I wish for?

2. *One is my dove, my perfect one is but one.***2** God so
loves the soul that gives itself entirely to him that he seems
to love no other; and from here he calls it his only dove.
St. Teresa after her death revealed to one of her sisters

1 "Ego diligentes me diligo." Prov. 8.17.
2 "Una est columba mea, perfecta mea." Song 6.8.

[152] that God has greater love for one soul that aspires
to perfection than for a thousand others that are in a state
of grace, but are tepid and imperfect. O my God, for how
many years have You invited me to become entirely Yours,
and I have refused! Death is already approaching, and shall
I die as imperfect as I have until now lived? No, I hope that
death will not find me as ungrateful as I have until now been.
Help me; for I desire to leave all things to become entirely
Yours.

3. Jesus Christ, through the love which he has for us,
has given his whole self to us. *He has loved us, and has
delivered Himself for us.***1** "If then," says St. Chrysostom,
"God has given himself entirely to you without reserve, if
he has given you all, and nothing more remains for him to
give you, as indeed he has done in his Passion and in the

Holy Eucharist, reason requires that you also should give yourself without reserve to him."**2** St. Francis de Sales says, "The heart is too little to love our bountiful Redeemer, who has loved us even to the laying down his life for us."**3** Oh, what ingratitude, what injustice, to divide our hearts, and not to give them wholly to God!

Let us then say with the spouse in the Canticles, *My beloved to Me, and I to My beloved.***3** You, my God, have given all to me, I will give all to You. I love You, my sovereign good. "My God and my all."**4** You desire that I should be all Yours, and such do I desire to be. O Mary, my mother, pray for me, that I may not love anything but God.

1. "Dilexit nos. et tradidit semetipsum pro nobis." Eph. 5.2.
2. Totum tibi dedit, nihil sibi reliquit.
3. "Dilectus meus mihi, et ego illi." Cant. 2.16.
4. Deus meus, et omnia.

[153]
MEDITATION 87.
The Trouble and Confusion of the Hour of Death.

1. *Be always ready: for at what hour you think not, the Son of man will come.***1** "Be always ready." Our blessed Savior does not tell us to begin to prepare ourselves when death has arrived, but to prepare ourselves beforehand; because the time of death will be a time of

confusion, when it will be morally impossible to prepare ourselves in a proper manner to appear for judgment, and to obtain a favorable sentence. "It is a just punishment," says St. Augustine, "upon him who, having it in his power to do good, will not do it, not to be able to do it afterwards when he desires to do it."2

No, my God! I will not wait until that time to begin a change of life. Make known to me what I must now do to please You, for I desire to do without reserve whatever You require of me.

2. The time of death is the time of night, when nothing can be done. *The night comes on, when no man can work.*3 The fatal news of the disease being mortal, the grief and pains which accompany it, the disordered state of the head, and, above all, remorse of conscience, will cast the poor sick man into such a state of distress and confusion as to hinder him from knowing what he is doing. He will anxiously desire to escape damnation, but will not find the means, for the time of chastisement will be at hand. I will repay them in due time, that their foot may slide.4

My God! I give You thanks for allowing me time

1. "Et vos estote parati; quia, qua hora non putatis, Filius hominis veniet." Luke 12.40.
2. De lib. arbit. Bk. 3, ch. 18.
3. "Venit nox, quando nemo potest operari." John 9.4.

4. Et ego retribuam in tempore, ut labatur pes eorum." Deut. 32.35.

[154] to amend, now that it is the time of mercy and not of punishment. I would rather lose all things than forfeit Your grace. My sovereign good, I love You above all things.

3. Imagine yourself in a vessel overtaken by a storm in the midst of the sea, already struck upon a rock and on the point of sinking; think how great would be your confusion, and that you would not know what to do to escape death. And from here imagine how great will be the confusion of the sinner, who at his death finds himself in a bad state of conscience. His will, his relatives, the last sacraments, restitutions to be made, the calls of God which he despised, oh, what a tempest will all these things create in the soul of the poor dying sinner! Go then, go now and put your troubled conscience in order.

O my God! let not Your blood be shed for me in vain. You have promised pardon to him that repents, where fore do I grieve from the bottom of my heart for the many offenses I have committed against You. I love You, O Lord! above all things, and will nevermore offend You. How is it possible I should ever again, after so many mercies, offend You? No, my God! I will rather die. Holy Mary, pray for me to Your divine Son, that I may never more offend him.

MEDITATION 88.
The Provoking of God by Sin to Depart from us.

1. Every soul that loves God is loved by him in return; and God dwells within it and leaves it not until he is expelled by sin: "He forsakes not, unless he be forsaken,"**1** says the Council of Trent. When the soul deliberately consents to mortal sin, it expels God, and as it were says to him, Leave me, O Lord! for I desire

1. "Non deserit, nisi descratur." Sess. 6. ch. 2

[155] to possess You no longer. The wicked have said to God, *Depart from us.***1**

O my God! I have then have the audacity, when I committed sin, to expel You from my soul and to desire to have You no longer with me! But You would not have me despair, but repent and love You. Yes, my Jesus, I do repent for having offended You, and love You above all things.

2. The sinner must be sensible that God cannot dwell in a soul together with sin. When therefore sin enters the soul God must depart from it. So that the sinner, by admitting sin, says to God, As You can not remain any longer with me, unless I renounce sin, depart from me; it is better to lose You than the pleasure of committing sin. At the same time that the soul expels God it gives

possession to the devil. Thus does the sinner eject his God who loves him, and makes himself the slave of a tyrant who hates him.

This, O Lord! is what I have until now done. Oh, give me some share of that abhorrence for my sins which You did experience in the garden of Geth-semane. Dearest Redeemer, would that I had never offended You!

3. When an infant is baptized, the priest commands the devil to depart from its soul: "Go forth, unclean spirit, and give place to the Holy Spirit."**2** On the con-trary, when man falls from a state of grace into mortal sin, he says to God, "Go forth from me, O Lord, and give place to the devil."**3**

Such is the foul ingratitude, O Lord! with which I have frequently repaid Your great love towards me. You came down from heaven to seek me, the lost sheep; and I have fled from You and expelled You

1. "Dixerunt Deo: Recede a nobis." Job 21.14.
2. Exi, immunde spiritus, da locum Spiritui Sancto.
3. Exi a me, Domine, da locum diabolo.

[156] from my soul. But no, I will now embrace Your sacred feet and will nevermore leave You, my beloved Lord. Help me with Your holy grace. And, O blessed Mary, most holy Queen! do not abandon me.

MEDITATION 89.
The Abuse of Grace.

1. The graces which God bestows on us, his lights, his calls, and the good thoughts with which he inspires us, have all been purchased for us by the sufferings and death of Jesus Christ. To the end that man might be able to receive them, it was necessary that the Son of God should die, and by his merits render him capable of such divine favors. He, therefore, who despises the divine graces, by abusing them, despises the blood and death of Jesus Christ. Such abuse has caused the eternal destruction of numberless Christians, who are now bewailing their sins in hell without hope or remedy.

O my God! how often have I deserved to become one of their number! I thank You that You now allow me time to bewail my past crimes, and hope that You will pardon me.

2. O God! what an eternal torment must it be to the souls in hell, to call to mind the many graces they received from You in this world, now that they know the value of them and the evil which they have done by despising them! My beloved Redeemer, give me light and grace to know my obligation to love You, for haveing, instead of chastising me for my ingratitude, and abandoning me to my sins, increased Your lights and redoubled Your calls upon me. Behold, since You now

call me, I will become entirely Yours, and forever.

3. Reflect, Christian, that if God have bestowed the same graces upon an infidel which he has upon you, that infidel would now most probably be a saint. And [157] what have you done? God has multiplied his graces, and you have multiplied your offenses against him. If you continue in your sins, how will it be possible for God to bear longer with you and not to abandon you? Put en end, without delay, to your ingratitude, and tremble, lest, if you should not now avail yourself of the graces which he bestows upon you, no more lights nor graces should be conferred upon you.

Yes, my God, You have already borne with me too long; I will nevermore despise You. And why should I delay? That You may really abandon me? *Cast me not away from Your face.*1 Reject me not, O Lord; from henceforth I will love You with my whole soul. You, indeed are most worthy of all love; and I will endeavor to please and love You in all things. Strengthen me and make me faithful. Mary, Mother of God, help me with Your prayers.

MEDITATION 90.
Divine Love Victorious over God Himself.

1. Our God is omnipotent: who then will ever over-

come and conquer him? But no, says St. Bernard, love towards man has conquered and triumphed over him:**2** for this his love has caused him to die in torments upon a disgraceful cross to secure man's salvation. O infinite love! unhappy the soul that loves You not.

2, What man, passing by Calvary on that day when Jesus was dying upon the cross, if, on inquiring who that criminal was, crucified in such a mangled state, had he been told that it was the Son of God, true God, equal with his Father, had he not been a believer, would he not have said with the Gentiles that to believe such things was folly? "It appeared folly," says St. Gregory, "that the

1 "Ne projicias me a facie tua." Ps. 1.13.
2 "Triumphat de Deo amor." *In Cant.* s. 64.

[158] author of life should die for men."**1** If it would have appeared folly to suppose that a king would become a worm for the love of a worm; greater still would have appeared the folly of believing that God have become man for the love of man, to die for man. This led St. Mary Magdalen of Pazzi to say, concerning this immense love of God, "My Jesus, You love us to infatuation."

And, alas! I, a miserable sinner, have not loved God, but have many times offended him!

3. Christian, lift up your eyes, and behold that afflicted one upon the cross, oppressed with grief and torments,

struggling in his agony, on the point of expiring, dying for the pure love of you. Know you who he is? He is your God. And if you believe that he is Your God, ask who has reduced him to such a miserable condition. "What has done this?"2 says St. Bernard. "Love has done it, regardless of its own dignity." : It was love, which refuses no pain, nor disgrace, when it would make itself known and exert itself for its beloved.

Jesus! it was because You did so much love me, that You did suffer so much for me: If you had loved me less You would have suffered less. I love You, my dear Redeemer, with my whole heart. And how can I refuse God my whole love, when he has not refused me his precious blood, his life? I love You, O Jesus, my love, my all! Holy Mary, Virgin of virgins, help me by Your prayers faithfully to love Jesus.

MEDITATION 91.
The Sentence of the Wicked at the Last Judgment.

1. Consider how great the rage of the wicked will be, to behold on the last day, the just, shining with glory,

1 "Stultum visum est, ut pro hominibus Auctor vitae moreretur."
St. Greg. *hom. 6 in Evang.*
2 Quis hoc fecit?
3 "Amor, dignitatis nescius." *In Cant.* s. 64.

[159] waiting with joyful eagerness for that *Come, you bles-sed,*1 with which Jesus Christ will invite them into heaven; and how great the shame and confusion of the wicked will be to behold themselves surrounded by devils, and trembling with expectation of that *Depart from me, you cursed*2 with which Jesus Christ will pronounce their condemnation before the whole world. O my dear Redeemer! permit not Your death, which You did undergo with so much love, to become of no avail to me.

2. *Depart from me, you cursed, into everlasting fire.*3 Such will be the sentence of condemnation, such the unhappy doom, which will fall upon the wicked: to burn forever in the flames of hell, accursed of God and separated from him. Do Christians believe that there is a hell? How is it, then, that so many voluntarily expose themselves to its terrible torments? O my God! who knows but that I also may be of their number at the last day? I hope through Your precious blood that so dreadful an evil will not be-fall me; but who will make me certain of this? Enlighten me, O Lord! and make known to me what I must do to escape Your wrath, which I have until now so often pro-voked; take You pity on me and forgive me.

3. At last, in the midst of the valley of Josaphat, the earth will open and swallow up the wicked, together with the devil and all his evil spirits; who will all hear those gates shut over them which will never again be opened for all eternity. O accursed sin, to what a mis-

erable end will You one day conduct innumerable souls! Unhappy they for whom is reserved such a lamentable doom for all eternity! O my God! what will my lot be? The fire of hell does not terrify me so much as the thought of being forever separated and at

1 Venite, benedicti.
2 Discedite, maledicti.
3 "Discedite a me, maledicti, in ignem aeternum." Matt. 25.41.

[160] a distance from You, my only good. My dear Redeemer, if until now I have despised You, I now love You above all things and with my whole heart. I know that the punishment of remaining forever separated from You will not befall those who love You; grant therefore that I may love You forever; bind me and unite me closely to You; unite me daily more and more to You, that I may never be separated from You, and then do with me whatever else You please. Holy Mary, advocate of sinners, never cease to protect me.

MEDITATION 92.
The Sentence of the Elect.

1. Come, you blessed of my Father.**1** Such will be the glorious sentence which in the day of triumph will be pronounced in favor of those who have loved God. St. Francis of Assisi, having had it revealed to him that he was one of the predestined, almost died of the consola-

tion which such a revelation afforded him; what then will be the joy of the elect when they hear Jesus Christ inviting them, Come, you blessed children, come and possess the inheritance of your divine Father; come and reign with him forever in heaven!

How often, O God! have I through my own fault forfeited Your blessed kingdom! But, O Jesus! Your precious merits encourage me to hope that I shall regain it. My dear Redeemer, I trust in You and love You.

2. Oh, how will the blessed congratulate one another when they behold themselves placed upon thrones and united in the enjoyment of God for all eternity, without the least fear of ever being again separated from him! What joy and glory will be theirs to enter on that day crowned into heaven, singing together songs of glad-

1. "Venite, benedicti Patris mei." Matt. 25.34.

[161] ness and the sweet praises of God! Happy souls, that are destined to such a blessed lot!

O God of my soul! bind me to You with the sweet bonds of Your holy love, that in that day I may enter into Your kingdom and praise and love You forever. *The mercies of the Lord I will sing forever.*1

3. Let us arouse our slumbering faith. It is certain

that we shall one day be judged, and that we shall receive sentence either of eternal life or of eternal death. If we be not secure of obtaining the sentence of life, let us endeavor to make it certain. Let us fly from all those occasions which might expose us to the loss of our souls; and unite ourselves to Jesus Christ by frequently approaching the sacraments, by pious meditations, by spiritual reading and continual prayer. The adoption or neglect of these means will be the sign of our salvation or of our perdition.

My beloved Jesus, and my Judge, I hope through Your precious blood that You will on that day bless me; and from here do You bless me now, and pardon me all the offenses I have committed against You. Grant me to hear the same consoling words that You did address to Magdalen, *Your sins are forgiven You.*2 I am sorry with my whole heart for having offended You; pardon me, and at the same time give me grace always to love You. I love You, my sovereign good; I love You more than myself, my treasure, my love, my all. *You are the God of my heart, and my portion forever.*3 O my God! You only do I desire. Holy Mary, by Your powerful intercession You can procure my salvation, and You desire it; in You do I confide.

1 "Misericordias Domini in aeternum cantabo, in aeternum cantabo." Ps. 88.
2 "Remittuntur tibi peccata." Luke 7.48.
3 "Deus cordis mei, et pars mea Deus in aeternum." Ps. 72.26.

MEDITATION 93.
The Dishonoring of God by Sin.

1. *By transgression of the law You dishonor God.*1
Take notice, sinner, what the Apostle says, and consider
what you do when you break the divine law; you dishonor God. Yes, the sinner dishonors God when he
loses all respect for him before his face, and declares by
his actions that it is not a great evil to disobey God and
to make no account of his law.

Behold, O God! prostrate at Your feet an ungrateful
sinner, who, after having been so loved and favored by
You, has many times dishonored You by breaking Your
precepts. I have deserved a thousand hells, but remember
that You died in order to save me from hell.

2. The sinner dishonors God by preferring a miserable
gratification, a wretched worldly gain, or a mere caprice
to the grace of God; for by giving his consent to sin he
declares that such things are more precious to him than
the friendship of God. Thus is God dishonored and
affronted by the sinner, who by his actions pronounces
him to be viler than some wretched gratification, for
which he turns his back upon him.

O my God! You are an infinite good; and how could
I, a miserable worm, prefer any corrupt inclinations and

passions to You? If I did not know that You have promised pardon to those who repent, I should not dare to crave Your mercy. I am sorry, O infinite goodness! for having offended You.

3. God is our last end, for he has created us to serve and love him in this world, that we may be happy with him forever in the next. But when man prefers a vile pleasure to divine grace, he makes his pleasure his last

1 "Per praevaricationem legis, Deum inhonoras." Rom. 2.23.

[163] end, he makes it his God. What a dishonor must it be to God, who is infinitely good, to see himself exchanged for something so vile and wretched!

My beloved Redeemer, I have offended You; but You would not have me despair Your mercy; although You know my ingratitude, yet do You love me and desire my salvation. I am sensible of the evil I have done by offending You, and I am sorry for it with my whole heart. I am resolved rather to die than again incur Your displeasure. I fear my own weakness, but I hope, in Your goodness, that You will enable me to be faithful to You till death. O Jesus! You are my hope and my love. Holy Mary, intercede for me, that I may obtain salvation.

MEDITATION 94.
The Joy of Jesus Christ at Finding the Lost Sheep.

1. Our blessed Savior says of himself, in St. Luke
(chap. 15), that he is the affectionate shepherd, who, having lost one of his hundred sheep, leaves the ninety-nine
in the desert, and goes in search of the one that is lost;
and finding it, receives it with joy, takes it on his
shoulders, and returning home calls together his neigh-
bors to rejoice with him, saying, Rejoice with me, because
I have found my sheep that was lost.**1**

O divine shepherd! I have been that lost sheep, but
You have sought me until, as I hope, You have found
me. You have found me and I have found You. How
shall I ever again stray away from You, my beloved
Lord? And yet such a misfortune may happen to me.
Oh, permit it not; never permit me, O Jesus! to leave
You and to lose You again.

2. But why, O Jesus! do You call together Your
friends to rejoice with You for having found the lost

1 Congratulamini mihi, quia inveni ovem meam, quae perierat.

[164] sheep? Should You not rather bid them rejoice with
the lost sheep for having again found You, its God?
But so great is Your love for my poor soul that You
esteem it Your happiness to have found it! My dearest

Redeemer, since You have found me, bind me to You with the blessed bonds of Your holy love, that I may always love You and may nevermore depart from You.

3. God, says the prophet, no sooner hears the voice of the penitent sinner crying to him for mercy, than he immediately answers and forgives him. *At the voice of your cry, as soon as He shall hear, He will answer you.***1**

Behold me then at Your sacred feet, O God! grieved from the bottom of my heart for having so often offended You, and craving Your compassion and pardon. I can no longer endure to behold myself at a distance from You and deprived of Your love. You are infinite goodness, and most worthy of infinite love. If until now I have despised Your grace, I now value it above all the kingdoms of the earth. And because I have offended You, I beseech You to avenge Yourself upon me, not indeed by casting me away from Your face, but by giving me such a sorrow for my sins as may cause me to lament my guilt before You, all the days of my life. Lord, I love You with my whole heart, and as I cannot trust that I shall continue faithful to Your love, be my help and my strength. And do You, O holy Virgin! help me with Your holy intercession.

MEDITATION 95.
Jesus Suffering the Punishment Due to our Sins.

1. *Surely he has borne our infirmities, and carried our sorrows.***2** Who could believe this, if divine faith did not as-

1 "Advocem clamoris tui, statim ut audierit, respondebit tibi."
Isaiah 30.19.
2 "Vere languores nostros ipse tulit, et dolores nostros ipse porta-
vit," Isaiah 53.4.

[165] sure us of it: "Surely he has borne our infirmities!"
Man sins, and the Son of God makes satisfaction for
him.

O Jesus! I have sinned, and have You made satisfaction for me? Yes, I have deserved hell, and You, in
order to deliver me from eternal death, have been pleased
to be condemned to death upon the cross! In a word,
in order to pardon me You would not pardon Yourself, and shall I ever be so base as to offend You again
during the remainder of my life? No, my Savior, I
owe You too much, I am too much obliged to love You.
Behold I am Yours, do with me what You please; I
will endeavor to please You in all things.

2. *He was wounded for our iniquities, he was bruised for
our sins.***1** Behold, my soul, behold your God scourged at
a pillar in Pilate's hall, crowned with thorns, wounded
from head to foot, and his whole body mangled and

streaming with blood; hear how he lovingly says to you, My son, see what you have cost me.

Ah, my sweet Savior! You have suffered so much for me, and how could I have repaid all Your love with so many offenses! You, to save me from being lost, have suffered so many torments, and I have lost You for a mere nothing! O accursed sinful pleasures! I hate and detest you; you have been the cause of all the sufferings of my Savior for me.

3. St. Margaret of Cortona, when she meditated on the sufferings of Christ, could not restrain herself from excessively bewailing her sins. One day her confessor said to her, "Margaret, cease to weep; for God has pardoned You." But hear what the penitent sinner answered: "Ah, Father, how can I think of no longer bewailing my sins, while I remember that they afflicted my dear Redeemer during the whole of his life?"

1 "Ipse autem vulneratus est propter iniquitates nostras, attritus est propter scelera nostra." Isaiah 53. 5.

[166]
My beloved Jesus, I also must have afflicted You during Your life by my sins. St. Margaret knew how to bewail her sins and to love You; but when shall I begin really to bewail mine, when shall I begin really to love You? I am sorry, my sovereign good, for having afflicted You. I love You, my dear Redeemer, more

than myself. Oh, draw my whole heart to You, and in flame it entirely with Your holy love; permit me not to live any more ungrateful for the many graces which You have bestowed upon me. Holy Mary, You can power- fully assist me by Your holy intercession to become holy; do this, I beseech You, for the love of Jesus Christ.

MEDITATION 96.
The Happiness of Possessing the Grace of God, and the Misery of being Deprived of it.

1. *Man knows not the value of divine grace,***1** and from here he exchanges it for a mere nothing. *It is a treasure of infinite value.***2** The Gentiles said it was impossible for a creature to become the friend of God. But, no; divine grace induces God to call the soul that possesses it his friend:**3** *You are My friends,***4** said our Blessed Savior to his disciples.

When, therefore, O God! my soul was in the state of grace, it was Your friend; but by sin it became the slave of the devil, and Your enemy. I give You thanks for affording me time to recover Your grace. I am sorry, O Lord! with my whole heart, for having lost it; in Your pity, restore it to me, and permit me not to lose it any more.

2. How truly fortunate should that man esteem himself

1 "Nescit homo pretium ejus." Job 28.13.
2 "Infinitus enim thesaurus est hominibus." Wis. 7.14.
3 "Surge, propera, amica mea." Cant. 2.10.
4 "Vos amici mei estis." John 15.14.

[167] who becomes the friend of his king! It would be presumption for a vassal to expect that his prince should make him his friend; but it is not presumption for the soul to aspire to be the friend of God. "If I would become a friend of Caesar," said a certain courtier, as St. Augustine relates, "I should have great difficulty in becoming such; but if I would become the friend of God, I am already his friend."**1** An act of contrition and of love makes us the friends of God. St. Peter of Alcantara said, "No tongue can express the greatness of the love of Jesus for a soul in the state of his grace."

My God! am I in Your grace or not? I certainly know that at one time I have lost it, and who knows whether I have regained it? O Lord! I love You, and am sorry for having offended You; make haste to pardon me.

3. Oh, how great, on the contrary, is the misery of a soul that is fallen from the state of grace! It is separated from the sovereign good. It belongs no more to God, and God belongs no more to it. It is no longer loved by God, but hated and abhorred by him. Before, he blessed it as his child; but now, he curses it as his enemy.

Such is the unhappy state in which I was, O God! when I have forfeited Your grace. I hope I have arisen from my unhappy condition, but if I have not, hasten, O Jesus! to rescue me from it. You have promised to love those who love You.**2** I love You, my sovereign good; do love me; and may I never again be deprived of Your love. Holy Mary, attend to me, Your humble client; I commend myself to Your patronage.

1 "Amicus autem Dei, si voluero, ecce nunc fio." *Conf.* Bk. 8, ch. 6.
2 "Ego diligentes me diligo." Prov. 8. 17.

[168]
MEDITATION 97.
Conformity to the Will of God.

1. The first effect of love is the union of will. The most high God, because he loves us, would have us love him, and from here he demands our hearts, that is, our wills: *My son, give me Your heart.***1** Our whole life and salvation depend upon uniting our wills to the will of God, which is the only rule of what is just and perfect: *"Life,"* says the Psalmist, *"is in his will."***2** He who is united with the will of God lives and is saved; but he, who separates himself from it dies and is lost.

No, my God, I will never more separate myself from whatever You desire of me. Give me grace to love You, and dispose of me as You please.

2. This is the great object of all those who love God, to conform themselves at all times to his divine will. And this is what Jesus taught us to pray for, that we may be able to fulfill the will of God here upon earth, with as much perfection as the blessed do in heaven. *Your will be done on earth, as it is in heaven.***3** St. Teresa made an offering of her will to God, at least fifty times everyday; in this imitating David, who said, *My heart is ready, O God, my heart is ready.***4** Ah! how effectively does one perfect act of conformity to the will of God change the sinner into a saint, as it happened to St. Paul, who by only saying to God, *Lord, what will You have me to do,***5** from a persecutor of the Church was changed into an apostle and vessel of election. O my God! I will never more lament the tribulations which You may send

1 "Praebe, fili mi, cor tuum mihi." Prov. 23.26.
2 "Et vita in voluntate ejus." Ps. 29.6.
3 Fiat voluntas tua, sicut in coelo et in terra.
4 "Paratum cor meum, Deus, paratum cor meum." Ps. 56.8.
5 "Domine, quid me vis facere?" Acts 9.6.

[169] me. I know that all will be for my good. I will say always, Lord, may Your holy will be ever accomplished. As You will, so do I will. Your will be done. As it has pleased the Lord, so be it done.**1**

3. The most certain sign that the soul loves God is its peaceful conformity to the will of God in all adverse oc-currences, such as poverty, sickness, losses, and ruin. In

the afflictions which happen to us from the malice of men, we should consider not the stone which strikes us, but the hand of God who casts it. God does not will the sin of those who deprive us of our goods, reputation, or life; but that we should accept such afflictions as coming from his hands, and should say as Job did when his goods were taken from him, *The Lord gave, and the Lord has taken away: as it has pleased the Lord, so it is done; blessed be the name of the Lord.***2**

My God! I have not acted in this manner; how often, to follow my own will have I despised Yours! But then I did not love You; now I do love You more than myself; I embrace all Your divine arrangements, and desire to do whatever You please. But You know my weakness, enable me therefore by Your assistance to accomplish what I now resolve. O holy will of God! You shall be from henceforward my whole love. Holy Mary, obtain for me the grace ever to do the will of God during the remainder of my life.

1 "Fiat voluntas tua. Ita, Pater; quoniam sic fuit placitum ante te." Matt. 11.26.
2 "Dominus dedit, Dominus abstulit; sicut Domino placuit, ita factum est; sit nomen Domini benedictum." Job 1.21.

Printed in Great Britain
by Amazon

44194142R00126